Rediscovering the Roots of Chinese Thought

Laozi's Philosophy

CHEN Guying

Contemporary Chinese Scholarship in Daoist Studies

Center for Daoist Studies, Peking University
北京大学道家研究中心

Three Pines Press
PO Box 530416
St. Petersburg, FL 33747
www.threepinespress.com

Lao Zhuang xinlun 老庄新论, translated by Paul D'Ambrosio

Funding for this translation was provided by Mr. Kong Xiangping 孔祥平 of Yuanlianhe Real Estate. Management and interface coordination was supplied by Ms. Wang Lina 王丽娜.

9 8 7 6 5 4 3 2 1

First Edition, 2015 – Printed in the United States of America

◎ This edition is printed on acid-free paper that meets the American National Standard Institute Z39.48 Standard.
Distributed in the United States by Three Pines Press.

Cover art: Chinese traditional landscape. Designed by Li Huanhuan and Brent Cochran.

Library of Congress Cataloging-in-Publication Data
Chen, Guying, author.
[Lao Zhuang xin lun. English]
Rediscovering the roots of Chinese thought : Laozi's philosophy / Guying Chen. -- First edition.
pages cm. -- (Contemporary Chinese scholarship in daoist studies)
Includes bibliographical references and index.
ISBN 978-1-931483-61-2 (alk. paper)
1. Laozi. 2. Zhuangzi. I. Title.
BL1930.C52813 2015
181'.114--dc23

2014032745

Rediscovering the Roots of Chinese Thought

Contents

Preface vi

1. Laozi before Kongzi 1

Laozi as Kongzi's Teacher 1

Laozi before *Lunyu* 9

Modern Scholarship 14

Laozi's Influence on Mozi 22

Conclusion 28

2. Laozi's and Kongzi's Teachings 30

Naturalism versus Rule by Virtuosity 31

The Importance of Society 34

Heavens, Dao, and Virtuosity 38

Human Innate Tendencies 45

Humaneness and Responsibility 51

Conclusion 57

3. The Early *Laozi* 63

The Guodian Versions 64

Moral Values 67

Philosophical Development 74

Issues in the Guodian *Laozi* 80

4. Laozi's Thought 88

Dimensions of Dao 88

Practical Application 96

Ontology and Experience 107

5. Laozi and Pre-Qin Philosophy 111

Mainstream Daoism 112

The Jixia School and Huang-Lao 118

Laozi's Impact 123

Conclusion 128

Bibliography 133

Index 137

Preface

The lifetimes of Laozi and Kongzi (Confucius) overlapped, Laozi being senior by about two decades and penning his eponymous work long before the compilation of the *Lunyu* (Analects). These are facts of history upheld by evidence in the pre-Qin classics. Records of Kongzi asking Laozi about the rites exist in the works of a variety of pre-Qin schools of thought.

These two figures, unrivaled throughout history, appeared toward the end of the Spring and Autumn period (770-76 BCE). Confucius went on to become the hallmark of Chinese culture while Laozi arose as China's leading philosopher, pioneering ideas regarding the origin of the world and attempting to resolve questions of the creation of the universe and processes of change within the material world. His theory of Dao provided a comprehensive and systematic theoretical explanation of the world in both its knowable and unknowable aspects. In fact, all forms of Chinese philosophical thought—be it dialectical, systematic, image-based, or intuitive—trace their roots back to Laozi, while Kongzi's thought lacks Laozi's rich dialecticism and focus on essences and origins. China's "philosophical breakthrough" came with Laozi.

Pre-Qin texts are generally compilations of the writings of major thinkers and their followers, as is the case with the *Lunyu, Mozi, Zhuangzi*, and many other texts. Only the *Laozi* was the work of a single hand, written by this historical figure Lao Dan in the first person and presenting a concisely worded unified philosophical theory. Today's transmitted version of the text has been altered over the centuries in places, especially in certain specific wordings, by its transcribers. However, the majority of the text remains intact—an amazing feat attesting to the potency of its content.

The accumulation of misinformation that reversed the historical chronology of Laozi and Kongzi has survived nearly a century. The unearthing of the Guodian bamboo strips provides further irrefutable, material evidence discrediting claims that Laozi postdates Kongzi, and yet the depth with which this mistaken inversion has taken hold has led academics to continue calling for a revisionist rewriting of Chinese philosophical history.

My personal belief is that the crux of the problem lies in scholars' substitution of cultural history for philosophical history. Kongzi's teachings belong predominantly to the area of cultural history. Scholars of philosophical history, however, have unconsciously expanded his work and mixed it incongruously into philosophy. They have also intentionally sought to minimize the groundbreaking contributions of Laozi's teachings. A great deal of our mainstream academic discourse in this area therefore deserves significant reconsideration.

The historical facts of Laozi's life and text have become a focus of contemporary academic debate on which I have authored the several papers that provided the original content for this volume.

— CHEN Guying, Beijing, June 2005

Chapter One

Laozi Before Kongzi

Laozi as Kongzi's Teacher

Laozi 老子, a respectful title for the historical figure Lao Dan 老聃, emerged as China's first philosopher, with Kongzi following as second. The questions Kongzi deliberates focus mainly on culture and cultural history, leaving his philosophical development quite weak. Lao Dan, on the other hand, authored the *Laozi* (i.e., Dao*de jing* 道德经)—the first text in China to demonstrate a complete philosophical theory. This text, accordingly, predates Kongzi's *Lunyu*. Unfortunately, the dating of these two great thinkers and their works has been plagued by inaccuracy and subversion.

In the words of Luo Genze, "Unless all pre-Qin texts are to be ignored, the problem of when Laozi lived needs to be solved. If this issue is not resolved, it creates huge obstacles for reading all pre-Qin books" (1982, vol. 6). This view is absolutely correct. The academic world in China has been tackling this issue since the 1920s, and the specter of misdating survives to this day.

In the *Shiji* 史记 (Records of the Grand Historian), Sima Qian 司马迁 refers to Laozi's life numerous times. He records Laozi's birth in Ku county in the state of Chu, part of present day Henan province, as well as his engagement as royal historian to the state of Zhou. The *Shiji* also attests that Lao Dan authored the *Laozi*, a book that addresses the issues of Dao 道 (way) and *de* 德 (virtuosity) in just over five thousand words. Finally, Sima Qian and others wrote accounts of Kongzi asking Laozi about rites (*li* 礼). 20th-century philosophers such as Liang Qichao 梁启超 and Feng Youlan (aka Fung Yu-lan), however, suggest that both Laozi and his text postdate Kongzi. Today, scholars believe that multiple distinct voices and ideas exist in the *Laozi*, and argue that it was complied after Kongzi died. These various accounts are clearly mistaken, but their profusion and pervasiveness allow this fallacious view to dominate current intellectual discourse. The result is that all publications in China on the history of Chinese philosophy assume that Kongzi predates Lao Dan and the *Laozi*.[1] A thorough examination of the dating of Kongzi, Lao Dan, and the *Laozi* is clearly necessary.

Laozi's Life

Kongzi is said to have been born in the state of Lu 魯 about 551 BCE and died there around 479 BCE—dates that are probably quite accurate. The years of Laozi's birth and death have unfortunately proven harder to pin down definitively. The best research shows that Laozi was probably born around 570 BCE, about twenty years before Kongzi. As for his death, the *Shiji* records that Laozi lived a very long life—an idea accepted by many scholars and schools of thought, although the exact number of years is widely disputed.

Laozi's name, literally "old master," also encourages speculation as to whether or not he actually existed. In the *Shiji*, Sima Qian records, "Laozi, a native of Ku county in the state of Chu, had the surname Li 李, first name Er 耳, and style name Dan 聃" (ch. 63). Since the pre-Qin classics left no documentation on Laozi, this biographical sketch draws solely on Han dynasty sources. Closer analysis of Spring and Autumn period texts, however, shows that the surname Li did not exist when Laozi was alive, whereas the family name Lao 老 did. This complication arose from the changing pronunciation of the characters. The pronunciation of the surname Lao at the time was very close to or the same as that of the character *li*, which led to their later confusion (Gao 2011: 135). Laozi's style name, Dan, fell subject to a comparable issue in which the characters *er* 耳 and *dan* 聃 were mistaken or substituted for one another due to their similar or equivalent meanings (Li 1958: 3). Clearly, any pre-Qin mention of Lao Dan or Laozi refers to a single person.

In *A Short History of Chinese Philosophy* (1997), Feng supposes that Lao Dan and Li Er are two separate people. He envisions Lao Dan as a

---

[1] Despite the majority of recent Chinese scholarship having shifted the dating of Laozi to follow Kongzi and sometimes even Mengzi, our first history of Chinese philosophy, authored by Hu Shi in 1919, places Laozi as first among the great pre-Qin thinkers. Additionally, Guo Moruo has Laozi preceding Kongzi in his 1935 treatment of the development of pre-Qin cosmology. These two preeminent modern intellectuals insisted on the correct ordering of Laozi and Kongzi.

legendary ancient sage and Li Er as a Warring States period (475-221 BCE) scholar. However, these two descriptions are completely fabricated and without concrete textual evidence. Reading the two figures as a single person is a far more convincing interpretation for the reasons given above.

Also addressing this problem, Liang Qichao argues that Laozi appears in the *Shiji* as "one individual whose story has different embodiments: firstly as Lao Dan, who Kongzi questioned about the rites; secondly as Lao Laizi 老莱子, a hermit figure who also appears in the *Shiji*; and lastly as the imperial historian Dan 太史儋" (2009: 13). This argument results from an improper understanding of the premise and approach Sima Qian takes with the *Shiji*,[2] which records everything from hearsay and legends to actual facts and often appends stories of additional personages to its major biographies.

Understood properly, the Grand Historian's confused and cryptic distinctions between these figures become quite clear. He writes, "Lao Laizi is also from the state of Chu, and wrote fifteen chapters." The "also" here signals a distinct separation between Lao Laizi and Laozi. As just before this passage, Sima Qian notes that Laozi wrote a book with two parts, his mention here that Lao Laizi's book has fifteen chapters further distinguishes the two from each other. Sima Qian brings up Lao Laizi within his biography of Laozi not because the two are a single person, but as an appended biography—one of the author's characteristic stylistic practices. In addition to this, Sima Qian lists Laozi and Lao Laizi separately and as from different locations when he catalogues Kongzi's teachers. Liang Qichao has erroneously combined two persons into one.

The imperial historian Dan, whom Sima Qian also mentions in Laozi's biography, is said to have met Duke Xian of Qin 秦献公 "129 years after Kongzi died." Therefore, according to the *Shiji*, the imperial historian Dan and Laozi clearly did not live in the same time period. The *Shiji* also presents the imperial historian Dan as a sort of popular diviner in his dialogues with Duke Xian, which is clearly at odds with Laozi's identity as a "hidden sage" (*junzi* 隐君子), showing quite definitively that they are not the same person (Zhan 1982: 42-43). Sima Qian here places the two figures side by side and explicitly contrasts them in order

[2] Xu Fuguan agrees that, "From his *Zhongguo lishi yanjiufa* 中国历史研究法 (Methods of Researching Chinese History), we see that Liang Qichao really does not understand the *Shiji* very well, and of course this misunderstanding includes the *Shiji*'s biography of Laozi" (1963: 483-88).

to establish them as separate characters. Liang Qichao's theory relies on a misinterpretation of the *Shiji* that completely misses Sima Qian's intended meaning.

Kongzi Asks Laozi about the Rites

Sima Qian writes in the *Shiji*,

> Kongzi wanted to emulate the Zhou dynasty, and so he asked Laozi about the rites.
>
> Laozi replied, "The people you are talking about are all dead, their bones turned to ash and their words all that is left. The sage that goes along with the times can control things, whereas one who does not harness the times moves aimlessly without purpose.
>
> "I have inquired into this and found that the sage keeps what is truly worthwhile hidden, as if it is empty. The sage's virtuosity is overflowing, although he appears to be an idiot. He rids himself of arrogance and excessive desires, expelling arrogance and wanton ambition. None of these things benefit the body of the sage." (ch. 63)

For the most part, the *Shiji* is consistent and accurate. Sima Qian's description of Laozi's comments, especially the section on keeping valuable things hidden and dispelling excessive desires, are completely in line with the content of the *Laozi*. It is therefore highly likely that the discussion the *Shiji* relates between Kongzi and Laozi regarding the rites actually happened.

Furthermore, Sima Qian was not the only person to record this event. Other pre-Qin texts, such as the Daoist classic the *Zhuangzi* 庄子 (Book of Master Zhuang), the Confucian record of official Zhou ritual, the *Liji* 礼记 (Book of Rites), and the *Lüshi chunqiu* 吕氏春秋 (Spring and Autumn Annals of Master Lü), a text influenced by many different schools, all include this exchange.

Laozi appears sixteen times in the *Zhuangzi*, eight of which describe the relationship between Laozi and Kongzi. In the "Tiandi" 天地 chapter (ch. 12), Laozi and Kongzi discuss "the utmost way" (*zhidao* 至道). In the "Tindal" 天道 chapter (ch. 13), the two discourse on the ancient classics of the *Shijing* 诗经 (Book of Songs), *Shangshu* 尚书 (Book of History), *Yijing* 易经 (Book of Changes), and *Liji*, as well as debate the central Confucian virtues humanness (*ren* 仁) and responsibility (*yi* 义). In the "Tianyun" 天运 chapter (ch. 14), they again discuss these along with Dao and the Six Classics.

The "Tianzifang" 田子方 chapter (ch. 21) tells of Laozi and Kongzi philosophizing about cosmology, literally, the "heavenly Dao" (*tiandao* 天道). They talk about all phenomena (*tiandi wanwu*天地万物) and autopoietic generation or spontaneity (*zifa xing*自发性) in the "Zhibeiyou" 知北游 chapter (ch. 22). As Xu Fuguan notes, within the *Zhuangzi*, "other than those who are completely fabricated, the relationships of seniority between historical figures are always well ordered" (1963: 78). The *Zhuangzi* mentions relationships and interactions between various characters: Kongzi and his followers, Huishi 惠施 (Huizi) and Zhuangzi, Gongsun Long 公孙龙 and Wei Mou 魏牟, etc. Examining them closely, seventy-nine prove to be distinctly possible and in accord with what is known of historical circumstances; only two are ruled out (Huang 1941: 1239). In other words, the *Zhuangzi*'s tales about Kongzi meeting Laozi, and the conversations they had, should not be taken as completely fictitious.

The *Lüshi chunqiu* combines the Daoist, Confucian, Legalist, and Yin-Yang schools of thought. It mentions Laozi in five places. First, the "Jiugong" 贵公 chapter calls Lao Dan "the utmost minister" (*zhigong* 至公) (1.4). The "Dangran" 当染 chapter records that "Kong studied with Lao Dan" (2.4); the "Quyou" 去尤 chapter states, "Lao Dan was independent, and never simply went along with common customs" (16.7). Laozi and Kongzi are differentiated in "Buer" 不二: "Lao Dan believed in being soft or gentle, whereas Kongzi advocated humaneness" (17.7). Finally, the "Zhongyan" 重言 chapter states, "The sage listens to silence and sees the formless. . . . This is Lao Dan" (18.2). These records, in addition to confirming aspects of Laozi's thought, also evidence the fact that "Laozi and Kongzi lived at the same time, and that Laozi was older," which scholars of the *Lüshi chunqiu* consider "beyond any doubt" (see Guo 1945).

The Confucian *Liji* also contains records of Laozi and Kongzi. The "Zengzi Wen" 曾子问 chapter includes four events involving Laozi, three of which feature Kongzi asking for the latter's explication (Kongzi stating, "I asked Lao Dan. . . "), while the other one relates Laozi guiding Kongzi in how to bury someone. These citations all show Kongzi seeking Laozi's direction in difficult situations. Xu Fuguan argues that these stories from the *Liji* "are different in content from their counterparts in the *Zhuangzi* and other early sources. The legends in the *Liji* are Confucian, and part of an entirely different tradition. Nevertheless, they generally coincide with each other in terms of the relationship between Kongzi and Laozi, suggesting that these stories are true." He also declares, "The *Liji* was probably compiled during the Han dynasty (206 BCE-220 CE), when the opposition between Confucianism and Daoism was quite palpable. If the four stories of the "Zengzi Wen" chapter about Laozi and Kongzi were from contemporary early Han Confucian scholars rather than pre-Qin sources, [they are unlikely to have been included]" (Xu 1963: 27)

We have now established that the three major pre-Qin schools of thought all record instances of Kongzi asking Laozi about the rites. Even texts biased toward Confucianism and critical of other schools, such as the *Hanshi waizhuan* 韩诗外传 (Mr. Han [Ying]'s Comments on the Book of Songs), recognize that "Kongzi studied from Lao Dan." The *Kongzi jiayu* 孔子家语 (Kongzi's Regulations on Family Relations) adds, "Kongzi asked Laozi about Dao." Evidence is found in all of these ancient texts that Kongzi and Laozi interacted, with Laozi being the elder master and Kongzi the student seeking the former's advice. There is no room to harbor any suspicion about this historical fact.

When, Where, and What Did He Ask?

Now that we have established that Kongzi asked Laozi about the rites, we should further investigate when and where this took place, and ask what actually happened and was said during these exchanges.

A range of possibilities has been asserted in response to the question of when Kongzi sought Laozi's advice. Some, like Gao Heng, believe that Kongzi was seventeen at the time. Gao argues that, according to both, Bian Shao's 边韶 *Laozi ming* 老子铭 (Inscription for Laozi) and Li Daoyuan's 郦道元 *Shuijing zhu* 水经注 (Commentary on the Waterways Classic; ch. 19), "Kongzi was seventeen when he asked Laozi about the rites." The *Chunqiu* 春秋 (Spring and Autumn Annuals) records a solar eclipse that supports this account (Gao 1979: 13).

A second answer is that Kongzi was thirty-four when he spoke with Laozi, which comes from the Qing-dynasty scholar Yan Ruoju 阎若琚. He calculated this by cross-dating the mention of an eclipse around the time Kongzi and Laozi met according to the *Liji* ("Zengzi Wen") with that recorded in the *Chunqiu*. Another answer comes from the *Zhuangzi*'s "Tianyun" chapter, which states, "Kongzi was fifty and still had not understood Dao, so he went south to Pei 沛 to consult Laozi."

Huang Fanggang 黄方刚 argues, "Laozi lived in Pei, as Zhuangzi states repeatedly. Pei was in the state of Song, which Kongzi visited often, making it quite plausible that he met with Laozi many times" (1941: 381). He therefore further asserts the possibility that Kongzi was fifty-seven when he met Laozi. In consideration of the mentions of eclipse in the *Liji* and *Zuozhuan* 左传 (Commentary of Zuo), he believes it would fit that

"Kongzi met with Laozi twice, first when he was fifty-one and again when he was fifty-seven" (Gu 1941, 381).

There are also four separate accounts about the location where Kongzi and Laozi met. Multiple passages in the *Shiji* state that Kongzi and Laozi met in the state of Zhou (near present-day Luoyang, Henan). The *Liji* places them in Xiangdang, which may have been in the state of Lu, i.e., Kongzi's home state (Gu 1941, 452). The "Tianyun" chapter of the *Zhuangzi* has Kongzi going south to Pei (near present-day Pei county, Jiangsu) to meet Laozi. Finally, the *Shiji* proposes that Kongzi lived in Chen 陈 for three years, and since Laozi was from Chen (the original state of Ku county), it is likely that they met there (Zhan 1982: 52)

These possibilities seem contradictory, and add to the suspicion some hold as to whether Kongzi and Laozi actually met. There is, however, no reason to believe that they only met once. It is quite possible that they met a number of times, and that several, not just one, of these accounts is correct. One could imagine, for example, that the meeting recorded in the *Liji*, when Kongzi is seventeen, happened when Laozi visited the state of Lu as a government official.[3] The *Shiji*'s record that "Kongzi tried to emulate the ways of the Zhou dynasty" and "Kongzi lived in Chen for three years," along with the *Zhuangzi*'s "Kongzi went south to Pei," present possibilities of the two meeting during Kongzi's travels in the middle and latter half of his life. Kongzi traveled to many different states looking for people to follow his teachings, and during these years, he very easily could have visited both Pei and Chen, meeting Laozi in either or both places. At that time, travel and communication were very difficult, which explains why different schools of thought would be familiar with only one or two occasions on which the two great thinkers met. The Zengzi school of thought (as recorded in the *Liji*), for instance, only mentions them meeting in the state of Lu, whereas the *Zhuangzi* only mentions them meeting in Pei. Thus, these different texts came to have stories that appear to conflict with one another, although in reality they may not.

Therefore, we find that at different times and places Kongzi received guidance on various topics from Laozi. The idea that there could only have been a single time and place where teaching regarding *li* was imparted appears fundamentally mistaken. Part of the reason so many

---

[3] Gao Heng (1979) believes that, when Laozi was around thirty-seven years old, he fled to the state of Lu to escape persecution by a local duke, where Kongzi had an opportunity to talk to him in 535 BCE.

scholars have assumed the two met only once is the consistent mention of the rites throughout multiple accounts. There is again no reason to assume, however, that they would have conversed over this topic on only one occasion.

The word for "rites" (*li*) can indicate formality in the narrow sense of a wedding, funeral, or graduation ceremony, but it also denotes something broader. A younger Kongzi seems to have been more focused on a narrower and more pragmatic understanding, inquiring about regulations, decrees, systems, and institutional policies. These included the placement of certain flags or memorials honoring the emperor during an army's march; funerals conducted on days of a solar eclipse; and how the burial of a small child ought to differ from that of an adult. These issues are all regulated by the rites, and therefore the scope of Kongzi's inquiry in his discussions with Laozi would not have been limited to a single conversation.

The *Liji* records Kongzi conversing with Laozi about the rites with regard to more mundane or pragmatic everyday occurrences. Other texts record Kongzi in the latter half of his life learning broader ritual principles from Laozi, including concepts such as the Dao of a full vessel (*teying zhidao* 持盈之道), which refers to the innate tendencies of all beings to reach extremes and then return.[4]

Most important in this regard is that Kongzi and Laozi possibly discussed the *Shijing, Shangshu, Yijing*, and other classical texts, which explore broad facets of culture and daily life, as well as specific and special situations. There is also the story of Hanxuanzi 韩宣子, who traveled to Kongzi's home state of Lu and, after reading the *Yijing* and *Chunqiu*, commented that these great texts fully embody the rites of the Zhou dynasty. This clearly shows that the content of the *Yijing* falls under the jurisdiction of the rites (see Liu 1986). The *Zhuangzi* goes on to state, "When Kongzi was fifty-one, he went to the southern city of Pei to ask Laozi about the rites. He asked about calculations [*dushu* 度数] and inquired about yin and yang"—the main topics of the *Yijing*. Kongzi's affinity for the *Yijing* in his later years, therefore, may have been inspired by Laozi, who had a much greater influence on later interpretation of the *Yijing* than Kongzi and who also greatly developed the *Yijing*'s cosmological aspects—an area that Kongzi seldom commented on.

---

[4] The texts even engage wording from the ninth chapter of the *Laozi* in so doing. See *Huainanzi* 12 sand *Kongzi jiayu*.

Laozi before *Lunyu*

The major activities of Kongzi's life were his teachings and traveling in search of a government to utilize his ideas. He never wrote anything by his own hand, himself asserting, "I transmit, but do not invent." The most reliable source of Kongzi's thought, then, is the *Lunyu*, in which his followers wrote down his teachings. It is likely that the text "was recorded by Kongzi's disciples within decades of his death and compiled into a cohesive text by later Confucian scholars—not written [by Kongzi's own hand] as his followers claimed" (Cui 1983: 321). This sits in contrast to the *Laozi*, which is Laozi's own work, and was written significantly earlier than the *Lunyu*.

Of the pre-Qin records that cite Kongzi, none references the *Lunyu*; later, the *Liji* does, but that text was not compiled until the beginning of the Han dynasty. According to Yan Lingfeng, the *Lunyu* "was put together sometime in the beginning of the Han dynasty, just before the Wen emperor set up scholarly titles [*boshi* 博士]" (Yan 1969: 523). Thus, the *Laozi* came much earlier, having been completed sometime before the end of the Spring and Autumn period. Zhang Dainian writes, "The *Sunzi bingfa* 孙子兵法 (Sunzi's Art of War) and the *Laozi* are stylistically similar. Since we can be sure that the *Sunzi bingfa* was written in the final years of the Spring and Autumn period, the *Laozi* may have been, as well" (Zhang 1979: 138). Yan Lingfeng further found marks of influence from the *Laozi* on the *Sunzi bingfa* (Yan 1969: 54).

The citations of the *Laozi* in various pre-Qin texts are further evidence that the text was already in circulation before the Qin dynasty (221-206 BCE). The *Zhuangzi*, *Xunzi* 荀子 (Book of Master Xun), *Lüshi chunqiu*, and *Hanfeizi* 韩非子 (Book of Master Han Fei) all cite the *Laozi* and comment on its ideas. Other classics also mention the *Laozi*, including the *Shuoyuan* 说苑 (Garden of Stories), *Taiping yulan* 太平御览 (Imperial Readings of the Taiping Era), *Zhanguoce* 战国策 (Strategies of the Warring States) and the *Zhongyong* 中庸 (Doctrine of the Mean).

In the *Shuoyuan* we find, "Shuxiang 叔向 said, 'Lao Dan has a saying, "The softest in the world overcomes the hardest in the world." He also says, "People's lives are soft and gentle, but their deaths hard and stern. The lives of grass and trees are soft and crisp, but their deaths withered and tattered.'" These sentences can be found in *Laozi* 43 and 67, respectively. Shuxiang lived during the rule of Duke Ping of Jin 晋平公, making him a contemporary of Kongzi. Thus, it is clear that the *Laozi* was already well known during Kongzi's time.

Taiping yulan 322 records, "Mozi 墨子 said, 'My defense proved effective against Gongshu Pan 公输盘,[5] because those who excel at conquering others make their strong points appear weak. This is why Laozi says, "Dao is like an empty vessel, and we must be sure to keep it from getting filled."'" Mozi here cites *Laozi* 4, so either he or his disciples must have read that text. Unfortunately, this section of the *Taiping yulan* also misquotes the *Huainanzi* 淮南子, making it less than completely reliable.

A citation from *Laozi* 39 appears in the *Zhanguoce*: "Although honorable or expensive, one must keep the petty and cheap as one's root. Although high [in position], one must fix one's foundation in the low. That is why kings and rulers refer to themselves as poor orphans or widows."

Finally, the Confucian classic *Zhongyong* reports, "Zilu 子路 [one of Kongzi's disciples] asked about strength. Kongzi said, 'Do you mean the strength of the South, North, or your own idea of strength? To be tolerant and gentle in teaching while refraining from taking revenge on others in ways that are not in line with Dao is the strength of the South.'" Laozi was considered the master of the "southern school of thought." The citation above, with its emphasis on being lenient and soft, is also exactly the rhetoric used throughout the *Laozi*, making it highly likely that Kongzi is referring directly to Laozi (Zhan 1979: 67).

Lunyu Citing *Laozi*

There are six major points in the *Lunyu* where the influence of Laozi's thought is especially notable.

1. In the "Shuer" 述而 chapter (ch. 7), Kongzi states, "I am like Lao Peng 老彭." Two interpretations of the meaning of "Lao Peng" lead to Laozi. Firstly, the "Lao" of "Lao Peng" could be referring to Laozi, as the character is the same, and the "Peng" to another person, Pengzu 彭祖 (of whom there are numerous records). This would mean the line should be understood as "I am like Lao and Peng." The other possibility, which is far more likely, is that Lao Peng is just another name for Laozi. Yao Nai 姚鼐 (1731-1815) writes, "Kongzi went south to Pei, in the state of Song, to meet Laozi. The city of Peng 彭 was near Pei, and Lao Dan once lived

---

[5] Translator's Note: Gongshu Pan, also known as Lu Ban 鲁班, was a renowned inventor of the state of Chu. He was convinced by Mozi not to attack the state of Song when Mozi was able to successfully ward off his attacks in mock situations.

there. That is why Laozi was also known as Lao Peng." Ma Xulun investigated this idea and concluded "Laozi's style name 'Dan' is often replaced in the *Lunyu* with 'Peng.' Kongzi's disciples recorded the character according to their own dialect, which is why it differs" (Ma 1974: 5). If this is actually the case, then we find a direct record of Laozi's influence on Kongzi.

2. At another point in the "Shuer" chapter, we find "Kongzi said 'I have yet to meet a sage [*shengren* 圣人]; . . . [the characteristics of a sage are to be] gone but as though still there, empty but as though full, frugal but as though extravagant.'" Scholars such as Li Taicai argue that this shows the direct influence of Lao Dan (Li 1958: 12). This passage is also strikingly similar to the line from the *Shiji*, where Laozi tells Kongzi, "a good merchant keeps his true wealth hidden, as if empty. When a sage's virtuosity is overflowing, he appears foolish" (63.2)

3.Tthe "Wei Linggong" 卫灵公 chapter (ch. 15) of the *Lunyu* records "Kongzi said, 'Did Emperor Shun 舜 not bring about order without exerting effort or intention [that is, govern through non-assertive action]? He did no more than sit on the throne [and everything proceeded smoothly].'" The concept of governing through non-assertive action (*wuwei*无为), i.e., non-assertive action, comes from Laozi's political theory. Indeed, non-assertive action is mentioned only once in the *Lunyu*, but the *Laozi* repeatedly uses this term, and even outlines descriptions of what exactly it means. This sentence is then proof of the *Laozi*'s influence on the *Lunyu*.[6]

4. A further example arises in the "Taibo" 泰伯 chapter (ch. 8), which relates, "Kongzi said, 'The manner in which emperors Shun and Yu 禹 governed was truly impressive. They possessed the whole world and yet acted as if it was nothing.'" This recalls the *Laozi*'s notions of "doing things without reliance" (*weier bushi* 为而不恃) and "not dwelling on one's accomplishments" (*chenggong buju* 功成不居).[7]

5. A comparison can also be drawn from the "Xianwen" 宪问 chapter's line, "Kongzi said, 'Humane people are necessarily courageous, but the courageous are not always humane'" (ch. 14), and the *Laozi*'s, "Feelings of kindness allow one to be courageous" (ch. 67). It is possible that

[6] Many scholars concur on this point, including Hu Shi 胡适, Huang Fanggang, Li Taicai, and Zhang Dainian.

[7] Translator's note: These lines are found in the second chapter of the *Laozi*.

the former was derived from the latter (see Huang 1941).[8]

6. A final place where we find Laozi's influence on the *Lunyu* is again in the "Xianwen" chapter: "Someone asked, 'What do you say to the idea that harm should be repaid with kindness?' Kongzi replied, 'Then how would one repay kindness? One should use justice to repay harm, and kindness to repay kindness.'" The original idea of repaying harm with kindness to which Kongzi responds appears in *Laozi* 63. This passage irrefutably shows Kongzi directly responding to ideas in the *Laozi* (see Zhang 1979).

These six points, and especially the last, clearly demonstrate that the *Laozi* was written before the *Lunyu*.

Intellectual and Cultural Contexts

Any suspicion about whether or not Laozi was born before Kongzi has already been dispelled. It is clearly a historical fact. This is why, as shown in the previous section, the *Laozi*'s influence can be found in the *Lunyu*. The dates of their origins and the way that Kongzi reacted to Laozi are extremely important for understanding the development of thought in China, as they are two of the most influential thinkers that this culture has ever known.

Regrettably, some scholars are bound by an extreme reverence toward Confucianism, coupled with ambivalence toward Daoism, which has created a prejudice that reversed mainstream academia's professed order of their two founding figures. This has tainted the long history of Confucianism's privileged status within China's academic world. Ever since Dong Zhongshu 董仲舒 (179-104 BCE) sounded the call to "respect Confucianism alone (*duzun rushu* 独尊儒术)," it has been popular for academics to be unduly partial toward Kongzi's thought.

Later, the Tang dynasty scholar Han Yu's 韩愈 (768-824) wholehearted support of Confucianism, particularly expressed in his *Yuandao* 原道 (Sources of Dao), led him to reject all other schools, especially Buddhism and Daoism, to the point that he ordered any text perceived to be in opposition or even at variance from Kongzi's teachings burned (see Huang 2011). Starting with Ye Shi 叶适 (1150-1223) in the Song dynasty, scholars began to question whether or not Kongzi truly learned from Laozi. Zhu Xi 朱熹 (1130-1200) even entertained the possibility that there

---

[8] Translator's note: The word *ci* 慈, "kindness," is often coupled with humaneness.

were in fact two famous thinkers named Lao Dan. However, later he changed his position to asserting that Laozi had become highly knowledgeable about the rites through witnessing corruption in the court while serving as imperial historian (Li 1986: 2997).

The 1930s saw a cresting of the wave of fashionableness for scholars in China to express doubt over the legitimacy of classical texts and their recordings. This happened under the banner of carrying forward old Confucian orthodoxy with Liang Qichao and Feng Youlan leading the charge and becoming the trend's most influential voices (Zhan 1982: 22). In addition to confusing the persons Lao Dan, Lao Laizi, and the imperial historian Dan, these scholars further disrupted the history of Chinese philosophy with their assertions that the *Laozi* was written after the *Lunyu*, *Mozi*, and even the *Mengzi* 孟子(Mencius).

There were, however, many scholars who sought to disprove Liang Qichao and Feng Youlan, including Ma Xulun and Zhan Jianfeng 詹剑峰. More recently, Xu Fuguan has also criticized Liang Qichao for too loose a reading of the *Shiji*, and Feng Youlan for "reading Lao Dan and Li Er as two separate people, as pre-Qin texts give absolutely not evidence for this claim" (1963: 29).

Feng Youlan presents two major arguments against classifying the *Laozi* as a pre-*Lunyu* text. Firstly, he supposes, "before Kongzi, books were not authored by single individuals," and secondly, that the *Laozi* was written in the simple classical (*jing* 经) style, which he says should chronologically follow the more dialogic (*wenda* 问答) style of the *Lunyu* and *Mengzi*.

This first argument fails immediately, as Feng assumes that the *Lunyu* was written by Kongzi, even though the master himself says, "I transmit, but do not invent." Kongzi definitively professes to never having written an original work, so the *Lunyu* cannot be of his own hand. More importantly, texts do in fact exist that were composed before the *Lunyu* and authored by a single person—compilations being more common but by no means the only form of authorship in ancient China. These include the *Zhuxing* 竹刑 (Deng Xi's Punishments), which was written by Deng Xi 邓析, and the *Sunzi bingfa*, authored by Sun Wu 孙武.

Scholars including Hu Shi have long since pointed out the shortcomings of Feng's second argument. Following the logic of postdating the *Laozi* according to its style would require to place the genesis of the *Shijing* similarly after the *Lunyu* and *Mengzi*—an utterly absurd and outright erroneous ordering. Therefore, in sum, Feng's dating of the *Laozi* lacks substantiation.

Liang Qichao's reverence for Confucianism, which has colored and shaped his biased historical accounts, is widely known in the academic world. Feng Youlan, though, even openly admits to having specific ulterior motives. "When I was writing about Kong Qiu [Kongzi], I had a goal in mind. I wanted to show that Kong Qiu was the first private educator, the first thinker to use his own ideas to develop a philosophical system, and the first founder of a school of thought. . . . I wanted to show him as a pioneer in these three areas. Accordingly, I had to dismiss other innovative thinkers contemporary to him" (Zhan 1982, 3). This is the motivation that drove Feng Youlan to reverse the order of the *Lunyu* and *Laozi*.

Modern Scholarship

During the 1920s and 30s, Chinese academics passionately discussed the historical significance of the Confucian tradition in Chinese culture. Many conclusions drawn from these debates have had a lasting impact on the relevant scholarship, but some of these contributions are misguided.

Unfortunately, it was popular at the time to question traditional dating and the legitimacy of classic texts. Professors enthusiastically hoped to prove that many pre-Qin texts were inauthentic. Among the most widely disputed were the *Sunzi bingfa*, *Yanzi chunqiu* 晏子春秋 (Spring and Autumn Annals of Master Yan), and the *Wenzi* 文子 (Book of Master Wen). However, the unearthing of ancient texts at Mawangdui and other sites in the 1970s buried any potential for the legitimacy of such arguments. Despite this, the *Laozi* and *Liezi* are among the few books that remain inaccurately dated to this day. Many contemporary scholars are still bound by the idea that the *Laozi* did not appear as a book until the Warring States period. The *Liezi*'s situation is even worse, as most have overlooked the signs of its pre-Qin origins and believe instead that it was written as late as the Wei-Jin period (220-316 CE).

After carefully analyzing the arguments for dating the *Laozi* as a Warring States text, I have concluded that there are basically two opposing interpretations. The first is most famously held by Liang Qichao and Feng Youlan, while the other is advocated for by Hu Shi and Zhang Xu 张煦. Liang and Feng both claim that the *Laozi* could not have been written before the lives of Kongzi or Mozi, while even more radical thinkers suggest that it was composed after Mengzi and Zhuangzi. The second camp defends the accuracy of the dating of the *Laozi* in pre-Han texts. These individuals systematically counter the arguments of Liang and Feng.

Judging objectively, the dozens of articles written on this topic by a wide range of scholars on both sides show the distrust of the *Laozi*'s traditional dating and subsequent call to push its formation to a later date to be untenable. This has unfortunately failed to topple the broad acceptance of Liang and Feng's position, which remains alive today and has continued to prove broadly influential.

The reasons behind this do not come from academia alone. Several years ago I met with Zhang Zhihan 张知寒 of Shandong University at an international conference on Mozi. When I asked him why hardly anyone has studied the *Mozi* since 1949 despite his views making him essentially an ancient Chinese Socialist, he replied, "One of the reasons for this is that Mao Zedong 毛泽东, in all of his writing, never once mentions Mozi. Another reason is that Guo Moruo, the most influential voice in scholarship, respects Confucianism and rejects Mohism. Under these conditions, it has been practically impossible to advocate studying Mozi!"

Zhang's reply made me think of the debate about dating the *Laozi* and the fact that those who date it after Kongzi and Mozi have remained influential for so long despite being clearly wrong. I figure the reasons behind this may be similar to the lack of study of the *Mozi*, which is due to the attitudes of certain influential individuals rather than characteristics of the actual text or history. After 1949, Hu Shi did not stay in mainland China, and his influence on mainland academia therefore all but disappeared, whereas Feng Youlan's grew dramatically. In 1958, Hu Shi lamented in the foreword to his *Zhongguo gudai zhexue shi* 中国古代哲学史(History of Ancient Chinese Philosophy), published in Taipei, that Feng Youlan's claim that the *Laozi* was written during the Warring States period "is truly illogical, and entirely without supporting evidence." Hu goes on to say that the misdating of the *Laozi* stems not from a lack of evidence but from "a problem of religious[-like] belief." It is precisely because Feng's misdating is based on faith and devotion to Confucius that his account has been so widely accepted. Very few academics since the mid-19th century have avoided mistakenly dating the *Laozi* after the *Lunyu*.

In 1988, I published an article on this, called "Laozi Precedes Kongzi." Afterwards, I broadened my studies to look at the *Huangdi sijing* 黄帝四经 (Four Classics of Huangdi; see Chen 2007) and Daoist texts of the Jixia Academy, including the *Yinwenzi* 尹文子 (Book of Master Yin

Wen), *Shenzi* 慎子 (Book of Shen Dao), and most importantly *Guanzi* 管子 (Book of Guan Zhong; see Chen 2006). I was surprised to find how broadly and deeply the thought of Laozi had influenced these Warring States texts. In order to have such an impact by the middle of the Warring States period, Laozi's thought must have already had passed through a significant period of transmission and study. As the transmission of ideas, and especially actual texts, was snail paced at the time, this would have taken quite a while.

The recently unearthed *Huangdi sijing*, written even before the mid-Warring States period, and the *Guanzi* both heavily reference the thought of Fan Li 范蠡—recorded the *Guoyu* 国语 (Tales about the States) section of the state of Yue—who was in turn directly influenced by Laozi. Fan Li had adapted Laozi's ideas to suit the end of the Spring and Autumn period. This added yet more support to the already overwhelming proof against moving the date of Laozi's life to a later period.

Additionally, from the perspective of the history of Chinese scholarship, deliberately misdating the *Laozi* as a Warring States period text has created a whole host of issues. Firstly, no one has made in-depth inquiry into the relationship between Laozi and Kongzi or the *Laozi* and *Lunyu*. Secondly, scholars are unwilling to look at the Laozi-based ideas in the *Sunzi bingfa*. Thirdly, today's sources show Fan Li to be an important link in the development of Huang-Lao Daoism, which arose in the early Warring States period and flourished in the middle of that period. Fan Li may have even been the founder of the Huang-Lao school, or at least a critical link between it and earlier Daoist thought. In either case, the misdating of Laozi and his teachings has prevented scholars from exploring Fan Li's relationship to Laozi.

Fallacious Arguments

The topic of the *Laozi*'s dating is an old one. Assertions that the text is post-*Lunyu*, however, have greatly disrupted research into the history of Chinese thought. Furthermore, several excavations of new textual resources have brought with them a number of pressing new questions. Scholars are therefore obligated to resolve these old but fundamental questions, which we can now explore from new perspectives.

Laozi's historical reality as a person is evidenced by many sources, including the *Zhuangzi*, *Lüshi chunqiu*, and various Confucian texts (especially the "Zengzi Wen" chapter of the *Liji*). Feng Youlan does not deny this, but rather follows Liang Qichao in asserting that Laozi himself, who lived during the Spring and Autumn period, did not write the *Laozi*. He claims that it was created later during the Warring States period by a follower teaching Laozi's thought. Most scholars today agree with Feng's position on this, but I find this explanation problematic in a number of aspects.

Firstly, Sima Qian's account in the *Shiji* that Laozi wrote a two-part text, totaling just over five thousand words on Dao and virtuosity quite accurately describes the *Laozi*. Supposing that the historical Laozi wrote a different text that was basically exactly the same as the *Laozi* is ridiculous.

Secondly, Laozi was a leading intellectual figure in his own time. Many texts attest to this. Even Kongzi expresses admiration for Laozi and declares to have studied with him. Why would one then assume that Laozi could not write an insightful text? He clearly was not lacking the intelligence or an audience with a demand for such a work. Furthermore, if the actual author of the *Laozi* was someone else, it is very strange that no trace of that person is found in any source whatsoever.

Finally, Feng's theory—heavily argued by Luo Genze (1941)—relies heavily on the assumption that before the Warring States period no text was authored by a single individual. Without getting into the many fallacies of this argument, simply the act of drawing a line at the Warring States period is completely arbitrary. Even if scholars could agree on when this period begins, it certainly could not be the case that once we enter the Warring States period thinkers are suddenly and miraculously able to author books themselves, whereas before this period they were unable to so. In actuality, there exist many pre-Warring States texts that were authored by one person. Above we already mentioned the *Zhuxing* written by Deng Xi. There are also Wu Yuan's 伍员 *Wuzixu* 伍子胥 (Book of Wu Zixu) and Fan Li's *Fanzi* 范子 (Book of Master Fan).

In many ways, the doubt that surrounds Laozi is analogous to a related controversy over whether or not Sun Wu truly existed and if so whether he is responsible for the *Sunzi bingfa*. Liang Qichao claims any text attributed to Sun Wu to be fake, and asserts that only records of authorship by Sun Bin 孙膑 to be genuine (2009). This matter was finally set straight in 1972, when bamboo scrolls containing copies of the *Sunzi bingfa* and *Sun Bin bingfa* as two different texts were unearthed at Yinqueshan in Shandong (Zhang 1992). In any case, the evidence against idea that texts were not independently authored before the Warring States period is overwhelming.

In his article, "On the *Laozi* Being Composed in the Late Warring States," Liang Qichao confuses Laozi with Lao Laizi and the imperial historian Dan, maintaining that the account of Laozi given in the *Shiji* is unclear—a conclusion that continues to mislead scholars to this day, and even a great deal of the English scholarship on the *Laozi* (1941).

Liang further argues that certain terms in the *Laozi* characterize it as a relatively late pre-Qin text. He maintains that the noble ranks *wanghou* 王侯 and *wanggong* 王公 "do not seem like terms that would have been used during the Spring and Autumn period," and that terms for humaneness and responsibility "were not a pair or used with the same level of importance before the *Mengzi*"(1941), which was composed after the *Lunyu*. Zhang Xu, among others, has already shown that Liang is mistaken here, yet again (1941).

In fact, the arguments about using *wanghou* and *wanggong* as terms for nobility and the coupling of humaneness and responsibility hardly require scholarly attention to be disproved. Already in the *Yijing*, which was written a few hundred years before the *Laozi*, we find the term *wanghou*. The coupling of humaneness and responsibility was well established prior to the writing of the *Mengzi*, as well. The *Zuozhuan*, a relatively early pre-Qin text, says, "It is according to the knowledge of ancients that humaneness and responsibility are praised over mere courage and strength." The *Guoyu*, while not coupling the two, also refers to the terms in parallel (1.15).the

The problem is not just that Liang and other scholars have made untenable arguments. Much more importantly, scholars made a severe, fundamental mistake when they created and promoted these fallacies to reject the traditional dating of the *Laozi*. Their misuse of logic commits "the fallacy of hasty generalization." Grasping onto a few words or a single piece of evidence to make broad judgments and conclusions is equivalent to asserting a general principle based on a single specific case. This violation of logic is committed frequently by the section of academia concerned with determining the authenticity of ancient texts.

After 1949, with the popularization of Hegel's theory of history, Chinese scholars began to commit a whole host of new mistakes on top of their earlier illogical and erroneous reordering of ancient texts. Hegel's system relies on a dialectical progression from thesis and antithesis to synthesis. In reality, however, the history of thought does not necessarily proceed along such a simple pattern. By stating that Laozi was necessarily reactionary to Kongzi's thought, scholars overlook the fact that humaneness and responsibility were important moral concepts in rites, government, and culture long before Laozi or Kongzi were even born. Laozi's supposed criticism of these concepts is in response to these traditional cultural establishments. Therefore, if Laozi served as a Hegelian antithesis, his opposition was aimed not at Confucius, but rather at the hundreds of years of abuse and corruption fostered by his society's traditional culture of the rites.

I should point out here that this was not a rejection or denial of morality. Laozi is merely expressing a divergent view and alternative set of values. We saw above that he is extremely concerned with sincerity (*xin* 信), kindness (*ci* 慈), and thriftiness (*jian* 俭) as ethical concepts. What he rejects is the rigid moral cultivation that lacks humanism, in its place advocating his own "natural" (*ziran* 自然; "self-so") values.

"Veneration of the worthy" (*shangxian* 商贤) was another well-established idea before Laozi and Kongzi's time. Laozi emphatically opposes this idea because during his life he saw it flourishing as a self-serving façade of morality for the aristocratic hereditary ruling class. Again, Laozi's "antithetical" push here is directed toward the social malpractices of his time, not Kongzi and Mozi's advocacy of "veneration for the worthy." The wording of the *Laozi* itself clearly addresses the ruling class directly. "Not venerating the worthy [or aristocrats] will lessen conflict among the people" (ch. 3). Here, opposition to venerating the worthy seeks to stymie its use to by the ruling class to propagate the idea of their greatness furthers.

In summary, three major ideologically driven methodological errors have resulted in misinterpretation of the *Laozi*:

1. Misunderstanding of the *Laozi*'s meaning;

2. misidentification of the objects of Laozi's criticism, which were the social phenomena of the Spring and Autumn period and abuses that Laozi associated with them; and most seriously,

3. the use of a single piece of evidence to make broad claims.

Misdating the *Liezi*

Before concluding this section, I would like to discuss the related question of the *Liezi*'s authenticity. Most contemporary academics agree without much reflection that the *Liezi* is a product of the Wei-Jin period, a time was rife with philosophical debate about Confucianism and Daoism. However, the *Liezi* contains none of the characteristic notions found in those discussions. The "Yang Zhu" 杨朱 chapter (ch. 7) of the *Liezi* is often presented as evidence in support of its Wei-Jin date. Firstly, scholars argue that Yang Zhu advocates indulging in desires, which was a popular, even hallmark, notion of that time. Secondly, they argue that Yang Zhu denounces traditional rites-based moral education (*lijiao* 礼教), also a popular trend among those thinkers. Therefore, they argue, the *Liezi* reflects social trends that did not occur until the Wei-Jin period.

The first point is easily refuted by simply looking at the *Xunzi*, which says, "Indulging in desires and resting in unbridled satisfaction of cravings is the way animals act. . . . [Such indulgence] is [the teaching of] Ta Xiao and Wei Mou" (6.2). Moreover, "Yang Zhu" does not really advocate indulging in desires. A quick glance at the *Zhuangzi* shows that the second point is unfounded as well. Already during the Spring and Autumn period, the rites were important enough for the expression "rites-based moral education" to appear in the *Zhuangzi*, a text that also often questions the moral validity of ritual practice. There is therefore no reason to suppose that the *Liezi* was a Wei-Jin text based on its rejection of the rites. Incidentally, the *Liezi* was written by followers of the Liezi school of thought, with which the "Yang Zhu" chapter does not necessarily fit. Its inclusion in the is due to the rather chaotic manner, in which many ancient texts were compiled and transcribed.

While Liezi certainly was a real person, he did not compose the text that bears his name. Like the *Lunyu*, the *Liezi* was written by disciples who recorded their master's words and ideas. Classical Chinese texts were often compiled section by section as collections of individual articles and not as whole works by single authors, as Yu Jiaxi outlines (1985). The *Laozi* is an exception to this, and is unlikely to have been a work of multiple authors, as it consists only of 5,000 characters and is therefore quite short as well as consistent in form and style. This brings major challenges to judging the authenticity of an ancient text, as well as to understanding the original ideas of early thinkers. It also means that each individual section of these works maintains a certain level of independence from the others. This makes it especially important that scholars avoid making sweeping judgments about an entire text based on several words or short passages, unless they are extremely central to the text or decisively significant (such as references to another text or idea).

Unfortunately, this type of unfounded generalizing is exactly what the scholars who deny the authenticity of the *Liezi* have done. Yang Bojun 杨伯峻 and other scholars in his camp take a few words or phrases as representative of the entire text in service of drawing rash conclusions. He is right in showing that some parts of the *Liezi* were written after the Qin dynasty, but this is natural due to the nature of the composition and transmission of such texts, and certainly does not mean the entire text was written that late. The detailed insights of Yan Linfeng's book on the *Liezi* (1994) and Xu Kengsheng's 许抗生 related work show quite definitively that the text was, for the most part, complied during pre-Qin times.

In fact, if we compare the *Liezi* and the *Zhuangzi*, we find that some passages in the *Liezi* were written later than the *Zhuangzi*, and others earlier. The *Liezi*, for example, records, "Liezi . . . returned on the wind. . . . His feet moved East or West, wherever the wind blew, . . . he did not know if he was riding the wind, or if the wind was riding him" (2.3). Likewise, the *Zhuangzi* notes, "Liezi rode the wind to move, light and elegant" (1.3). The *Liezi* passage seems to have been a source for the *Zhuangzi*. Additionally, the *Liezi* records, "Yin Tang asked Xia Ge, '. . . Is there any limit to the high and low or the eight directions?' Xia Ge replied, 'I do not know.'" (5.1). The *Zhuangzi* expounds on this, "Tang asked Ji the similar question, 'Is there any limit to the high and low or four directions?'" (1.2). Clearly, dating the entire *Liezi* after the *Zhuangzi* would be committing the same mistakes that have been used in attempt to push the dating of the Laozi forward. The *Liezi* was for the most part written before the Qin dynasty, with small sections altered or added by later scholars.

Righting the Dialectic

We have now seen that Liang Qichao, Feng Youlan, and others who argue that the *Laozi* was composed after the *Lunyu* rely on weak, superficial evidence. Nevertheless, and despite those who have proved this view mistaken, this unhistorical assertion has become a popularly held belief. Sadly, the majority of academics have followed suit.

This movement was bolstered by the popularization of Hegel's logic and theory of the development of spirit, which became extremely influential in China beginning in the late 1940s. Hegel's dialectic, especially the rhetoric and structure of "thesis, antithesis, synthesis," was incorporated into Chinese histories.[9] Frederick Copleston's criticism of simplistic interpretations of Hegelian theory proves highly applicable to its applica-

---

9 Translator's note: Using Hegel's model to understand history basically requires the *Laozi* to be written after the *Lunyu*. Many lines in the *Laozi* are read as being in direct opposition to the *Lunyu*. Kongzi is then viewed as the thesis, while Laozi represents the antithesis, and the Mystery Learning of the Wei-Jin becomes a representation of the synthesis.

tion in China. Copleston writes, "But if the history of philosophy is no mere collection of isolated opinions, it cannot be regarded as a continual progress or even spiral ascent. That one can find plausible instances in the course of philosophic speculation of the Hegelian triad of thesis, antithesis and synthesis is true, but it is scarcely the task of a scientific historian to adopt an *a priori* scheme and then to fit the facts into that scheme"(1993: 1-5).

Some scholars have used Hegel's theory to reinterpret the history of philosophy in China in just this way. They argue that, for example, Kongzi's affirmation of humaneness and responsibility must have existed before Laozi's supposed rejection, as well as that Kongzi's remark about promoting the worthy (*juxian* 举贤) or Mozi's comments about veneration for the worthy had to be known to Laozi before he would have proposed the opposite. This is mistaken. Humaneness and responsibility were influential terms even before Kongzi discussed them, and appear in records as far back as the Western Zhou dynasty (1122-771 BCE). By the Spring and Autumn period, they were even more popular. In the *Zuozhuan*, the word "humane" (*ren*) appears forty-four times and "responsible" (*yi*) over one hundred and forty-five. Laozi's dismissal of these virtues is given in opposition to the various malpractices of the late Spring and Autumn period committed under the guise of "ruling by virtuosity." Daoist criticism of Confucian thought did not appear until after the *Laozi* (e.g., the *Zhuangzi*).

Similarly, Laozi's arguments against revering the worthy (*xian* 贤) should not be confused as in dialogue with Kongzi or Mozi. The idea of "appointing the worthy" (*renxian* 任贤) is the most likely target of Laozi's critique, a term traceable to the beginning of the Western Zhou dynasty. The late 4th-century BCE chapter "Lizheng" 立政 of the *Yizhou shu* 逸周书 (Lost Book of the Zhou) presents the first treatise on this topic. In the Spring and Autumn period, the state of Qi's appointments of Guan Zhong 管仲 and Bao Shuya 鲍叔牙, along with Duke Wen of Jin's 晋文公 advocacy of "upholding the worthy and good as model people" (*ming xianliang* 明贤良), began a legacy of promoting virtuous elites that Laozi criticizes and Kongzi later supports. Again, misreading Laozi as addressing ideas in the *Lunyu* results in historical inaccuracy as well as in a misinterpretation of his ideas.

As for Mozi, he worked out his disagreements with Kongzi's position by expanding the proposition of *shangxian* to include a broader social range, advocating egalitarian meritocracy. Regardless of class or social background, the *Mozi* states, anyone of virtuosity should be promoted.

Laozi's Influence on Mozi

The *Laozi* impacted essentially every pre-Qin thinker. Evidence of this is found in almost all surviving texts from the so-called Hundred Schools flourishing at the time. The relationship between Laozi and Kongzi has already been discussed in detail, but there is much more to explore in the larger picture. In many regards, the relationship between the *Laozi* and the *Lunyu* looks relatively straightforward compared to that between the *Laozi* and later texts. While stories of the two masters' exchanges appear throughout Sima Qian's *Shiji*, there are also obvious references to Laozi in the *Lunyu*. As noted earlier, when Kongzi mentions Laozi's concept of "bringing about order without exerting effort or intention," i.e., "governing through non-assertive action" (15.5), this comes from Laozi's political theory. I have also already discussed how the *Lunyu* lifts the phrase "repaying harm with kindness" from *Laozi* 63.

Laozi's relationship with Mozi, who lived after Kongzi, on the other hand, is more difficult to trace. Even today, very few scholars have attempted to discuss this problem. Mohist scholars formed an independent school that launched pointed criticism on their Confucian counterparts during the Warring States period that focused especially on ethical and political ideas. While the *Huainanzi* claims that Mozi had a Confucian education (21.25), his true intellectual background is not in fact that clear. Looking at the *Mozi* itself, we find that he was known for having studied everything he could and also to have represented a lower social class of farmers and workers. Mozi most certainly became very familiar with Confucian texts; however, that did not preclude him from deeply studying the *Laozi*, as well.

Over twenty years ago, while working at Taiwan University, I taught a course on the *Mozi*. At the time, I was not particularly focused on the connection between Mozi and Laozi. During that semester, however, we often found ourselves using the *Taiping yulan* to establish that Mozi had read the *Laozi*. In a citation that may originally come from *Huainanzi* 12, it records, "Mozi wanted to defend [the state of Song], and forced Gongshu Ban to concede, but did so not through military prowess. Those who are good at winning rely on the weak to overcome the strong. This is based on Laozi's statement, 'Dao can be used when it is empty, and this use is limitless'" (322.53). The *Taiping yulan* thereby makes it clear that Mozi read the *Laozi*.

Continuing to study the *Mozi*, I gradually discovered that there are many places where Laozi's impact is apparent. The ideas of the two thinkers have much in common, and the *Mozi* frequently uses passages or concepts from the *Laozi*. These mainly appear in chapters often believed to be Mozi's earliest works, such as "Qinshi" 亲士, "Xiushen" 修身, and "Fayi" 法仪. Since there is little scholarship devoted to this subject, let me go through some examples.

1. The *Laozi* says, "He who has the mother [or origin] of the state can continue [to be in power] for a long time. This is called having deep roots and a solid trunk, and is the method [Dao] for seeing long life" (ch. 59). The *Mozi* uses similar language, "When advice has foresight and sternness, a state can be secure for a long time" (1.1.3). Not only are the ideas about governance related, but also many of the same terms are employed by Mozi, for instance, "long life" (*changsheng* 长生).

2. The first chapter of the *Mozi* also contains the line, "Thus it is said, 'The flourishing is difficult to guard" (1.1.5) In his *Mozi jijie* 墨子集解 (Collected Works of Mozi), Zhang Chunyi 张纯一 argues that the acknowledgment, "Thus it is said," refers to the *Laozi*. The *Laozi* records, "It is better to leave something unfilled than carry it when full. Rubbing a sharp edge will not make it last" (ch. 9). Both texts advocate preventing things from becoming too prosperous or full (*sheng* 盛, *ying* 盈), that is, trying to avoid conditions of extremes.

3. The *Laozi* says, "It is by not thinking of oneself as great that one is able to do great things" (ch. 34), as well as, "Large rivers and lakes are able to be so big because they are good at residing in the lower position" (ch. 66). Mozi borrows from these two passages when he writes, "Therefore, large rivers do not neglect smaller brooks and streams, and are thereby filled, and become great" (1.1.6)

4. Zhang Chunyi argues that Mozi is influenced by Laozi when he cites the *Mozi*, "The rulers of only a thousand people do not put themselves beyond the people's reach. They are straight as an arrow...and unable to tolerate myriad different ways" (1.1.6-7). The *Laozi* says, "The straightest appears crooked," which Zhang explains as referring to Dao in a deep sense: the greatest Dao or straightness accords with the various Daos and the straightness of the "myriad different ways" of things in the world, and therefore anything "straight like an arrow" is not great straightness. He cites Cao Jian's 曹笺 succinct explanation, "Anything too straight is unable to accommodate [the variety of the world]."

5. The second chapter of the *Mozi* also indicates the author's approval of Laozi. "When single tasks cannot be completed, do not take on many tasks. When in the dark about common things, do not pursue broad [theoretical] knowledge" (1.2.1). Zhang argues that if one compares this citation to similar arguments for prudence in work and learning in *Laozi* 23, 63, 64, and 81, the connection between the two texts in quite obvious.

6. Mozi writes, "[With] accomplishments, fame will follow" (1.2.4). This is quite similar to the *Laozi*'s statement that "accomplishments lead to fame" (ch. 9). Again, we find that the same terms are being used in the two texts. The *Mozi* continues, "He who is energetic but gets nothing done may work hard, but does not get what he desires" (1.2.4). The same language and message were already presented in Laozi's lines, "Not to get in one's own way—that is how to achieve success" (ch. 22) and "One who boasts one's own greatness does not succeed" (ch. 24).

7. In the same paragraph, Mozi writes, "Wise people can discern things in their heart-and-mind, but they do not speak a lot" (1.2.4). This sounds very similar to the *Laozi*'s idea that sages are often silent. "The sage resides in non-assertive action, and teaches without using language" (ch. 2). *Laozi* 5 and 23 also contain similar notions.

8. Mozi also appropriates Laozi's famous passage, "Humanity follows the earth, the earth follows the heavens (*tian* 天), the heavens follow Dao, and Dao follows nature" (ch. 25). Mozi himself introduces it as a cite, although he does not mention the *Laozi* explicitly. "Thus it is said, 'Nothing is better than following the heavens'" (*Mozi* 1.4.3). In fact, in this passage, Mozi not only promotes the idea that humanity should follow the heavens, but he also openly denies the importance of parents, teachers, and officials. He even emphasizes the impartiality of the heavens, another Laozi idea.

9. Although there are certainly many other references, the final one that I will mention is the *Mozi*'s line, "Prudence and thriftiness lead to prosperity" (1.6.9), which is directly related to the *Laozi*'s saying, "Thriftiness allows one to be broadly prosperous" (ch. 67)

The first four citations given above are all from the very first chapter of the *Mozi*, entitled "Qinshi." Although much of the text has been edited and added to, most scholars agree that Mozi himself wrote the first chapter. Zhang Chunyi writes, "'Qinshi' is not a recording of Mozi's oral teachings by his disciples, but rather the work of his own authorship" (Zhang 1936). Wang Huanbiao similarly writes, "['Qinshi'] may have had certain words added by later scholars, but it is, for the most part, all Mozi's own writing" (2005). While the following chapters present themselves as records of his thought by his disciples, "Qinshi" does not, and is very likely to be the work his own hand. This chapter also reflects clearly that Mozi not only read the *Laozi*, but also found the work's ideas highly influential.

Laozi was born around the end of the Spring and Autumn period, while Mozi lived in the beginning of the following Warring States period. During these years, rites, music, culture, and tradition began to deteriorate, and the two masters had much in common in the way they viewed this problem, particularly traditional Zhou culture and its rites-based political system. The *Huainanzi* summarizes Mozi's view as "Going against Zhou ways and advocating Xia politics" (21.25), and contemporary scholars have spent great deal of ink outlining Laozi's similar connection to Xia dynasty culture, Wang Bo among them (1989).

Mozi's reverence for the Xia, as well as his harsh criticism of the Zhou and advocacy of turning back to earlier culture, have many connections to Laozi. Zhang Chunyi points out that the *Mozi*'s inclusion in the Dao*zang* 道藏 (Daoist Canon) is due to the similarities of his and Laozi's thought. He also argues that Mohism accords with Daoism in rejecting ritual music, fate (*ming* 命), and overall Confucian principles in favor of valuing hard work, humility, simple living, and general equality among classes and family members (1936). Zhang's point here is well taken, as both Daoist and Mohist scholars promote thriftiness, approach problems pragmatically, advocate the plain and simple, and oppose the rites for the inconsistent valuation of different classes.

Daoists and Mozi held a very similar line in their opposition to the traditional cultural values that Confucians upheld. The corruptions that gradually crept into Zhou institutions had created social and political disorder, but Kongzi and Mengzi sought to reestablish them through education, believing society would thrive if only they were properly implemented. The Confucians were, however, basically alone in defending these customs.

Most pre-Qin thinkers took a negative view of Zhou ways, Daoists and Mohists being the most outspoken. The *Laozi* therefore reads, "The heavens and earth are not humane . . . Sages are not humane" (ch. 5). Here, humaneness (*ren*) refers to being partial or practicing favoritism. After all, this is exactly how Mengzi defines humaneness: "Affection for one's relatives, that is humaneness" (6B.23). It is this "affection" that Laozi protests, for he finds that it allows officials to practice nepotism, a major source of corruption in ancient China. Mozi's dismissal of this kinship-based favoritism is even more apparent. He writes, "Ancient sage-rulers [governed well] . . . without giving special consideration to relatives" (2.2.1). He goes on to say, "The [true] sage-ruler would not appoint a relative who was not capable. . . Family members who do not have the ability...should not be employed [by the ruler]" (2.3.2).

During this time, the rulers of the various states all sought to appropriate the possessions of the people to fund their extravagant lifestyles. Once again, both Laozi and Mozi share a similar perspective on this social phenomenon. Laozi repeatedly criticizes these rulers, writing, "As for those who wear elegant clothing, carry sharp swords, indulge in eating, and have an overabundance of things, these [rulers] are robbers and show-offs. They do not accord with Dao" (ch. 53). He goes on to say, "The people starve because of the taxes the rulers gobble up; this causes famine" (ch. 75). Mozi similarly writes, "Today's rulers harm the people in a number of ways. They exhaust people with work and implement heavy taxes. The people do not have enough money to live. They starve or freeze to death because of it" (6.1.3)

The two schools are also basically pacifist. Laozi writes, "An official who is in accord with Dao does not use military means to force the things of the world" (ch. 30). He continues, "Even the best weapons are inauspicious things, abhorrent to all. Those who know Dao do not use them" (ch. 31). Mozi is even more outspoken, and devotes an entire chapter of his book to this topic. The position he takes in his chapter *Feigong* 非攻, or "anti offensive war," is, again, almost exactly the same as Laozi's.

Laozi and Mozi also share in taking *tian* or "heavens" as a major philosophical concept. Mozi's focus on "the meaning [or purpose] of the heavens" (*tian zhi yi* 天之意) is comparable to Laozi's "Dao of the heavens" (*tian zhi dao* 天之道), and both borrow the idea of the heavens to express their philosophical views. The two are especially similar when they discuss their universality or plurality (*jian* 兼). Kongzi pays little attention to the heavens, but Mozi dedicates the entire "Tianzhi" 天志 chapter to their discussion.

The Mohists formed a unique and independent school of thought with clear hues of ancient socialist tendencies. While certain areas of their teachings were quite close to the Confucians, their rejection of traditional rites and the Confucian support of it is only one of many areas where they accord with the Daoists. Mozi's original view on the world clearly borrowed a lot from the *Laozi*, giving even further evidence for dating that text to the Spring and Autumn period.

Conclusion

Laozi's arguments against humaneness and responsibility as well as his ideal of the empowerment of "men of virtuosity," therefore, both targeted what he saw as problems with the thought of the late Western Zhou period. In fact, these terms and the importance attached to them (especially by later scholars) were formed through dialogue between the various schools of thought of the time. Stating a position on these issues is not necessarily useful in dating a text, since thinkers both before and after Kongzi discuss these terms and ideas. All of this renders a precise application of Hegel's dialectical theory, especially as a tool for dating, inapplicable.

Contemporary scholars who adopt Hegel's dialectic to construe Laozi's criticisms by directing them at the *Lunyu* and *Mozi* have completely misused Hegel. They perverse his theory by trying to find the root of social movements and ideas in books instead of investigating social structures. The latter project of understanding theoretical and cultural development through customs and social phenomena is what Hegel himself engaged in. This makes his ideas so important.

In addition to this, Feng Youlan further attempts to push back the dating of the *Laozi* on the basis that the text exhibits a complete philosophical system, claiming, "The *Laozi* summarizes the development of earlier Daoist theory" (1986: 256). A work cannot, however, be dated by the maturity and completeness of its thought. The development of scholastic discourse is extremely complex, and innovative thinkers often present systems of thought more expansive and penetrating than their followers' contributions.[10] This is a common pattern in both Chinese and other thought, and holds true for leading thinkers from Plato to Kongzi and Zhuangzi. Philosophy does not progress linearly like the achievements of science or math; it meanders and curves, developing with twists

---

[10] Hu Shi, in a letter to Qian Mu, once wrote about the difficulty of tracing the development of thought, pointing out, "Greek thought had already developed to a very deep state when Medieval Europe became suddenly stuck in a very coarse and shallow religiosity. . . . This is similar to later Mahayana Buddhism's descent into esoteric practices after Buddhism had already reached profound philosophical levels" ("Yu Qian Mu xiansheng lun Laozi wenti shu" 与钱穆先生论老子问题书).

and turns.

The *Yijing* scholar Chen Jinsheng writes, "Affirming that the *Zhouyi* [*Yijing*] was produced during the Western Han dynasty does not mean that the text we have now is exactly the same as it was back then. . . . As the *Zhouyi* was passed down, parts may have been added, deleted, or modified, making it in many ways a different text" (1982). The *Laozi* underwent a similar process, and the version we read today was modified and commented on as it was copied; however, the original *Laozi*, penned in Lao Dan's own words, nevertheless influenced texts like the *Sunzi bingfa* and the *Lunyu*.

In sum, the development of pre-Qin thought saw social upheaval against the widespread abuses of power that had developed over hundreds of years and were based on traditional ideas and cultural practices. Laozi's keen insight allowed him to criticize these traditions systematically, whereas Kongzi's more conservative approach aimed to preserve and improve upon certain Zhou dynasty practices. Mozi criticized Kongzi's approach to political reform, emphasizing the inclusion of lower classes, which produced conflict between Confucian and Mohist scholars. By the Warring States period, a number of schools existed, each advocating their own views on social institutions and customs. Their influence on each other as well as on later scholars proved pervasive and dynamic, unable to be captured by a simple linear dialectical system.

Chapter Two

Laozi and Kongzi's Teachings

Following the argument that many historians have been mistaken in their assumptions that Kongzi preceded Laozi, this section compares their theories, showing that Laozi was China's first philosopher and that Kongzi is more accurately honored as its first ethicist. The specific differences in their thought provide further evidence that Laozi's theory developed before Kongzi's.

Despite his limited access to Chinese texts, Hegel's lectures on history include many insightful comments about early Chinese thinking. He describes Kongzi's thought as a moral theory:

> Confucius is thoroughly moralistic and not a speculative philosopher. The heavens, the universal power of nature, which by the emperor's authority are an actuality, are linked to the moral nexus, and Confucius chiefly developed their moral aspect. His teaching coalesced with state religion. All the mandarins had to study him. However, the sect of the Dao based itself solely on abstract thinking. (1995)

Here Hegel seems aware of the well-established notion that the Chinese employ Confucian thought in official or public use and Daoism as its private or personal counterpart. More importantly, however, he touches on the difference between Kongzi and Laozi, noting that Kongzi is a moral theorist and Laozi more analytical.

Using a strictly academic perspective of philosophy, it is almost impossible to compare the two. Laozi developed a complete metaphysical system, whereas Kongzi's teachings contain very little cosmology or ontology. Laozi advocates "calm observation" (*jingguan* 静观) and "thorough examination" (*xuanjian* 玄鉴) as methods for understanding, but Kongzi essentially fails to address epistemology. Laozi even establishes a systematic theory that employs dialectical thinking, while Kongzi's method very much lacks in this regard.

These elements—ontology, metaphysics, epistemology, and dialectics—constitute the core of any philosophy, and comparing the two, we find that Laozi's thought is rich in each, and Kongzi's mostly devoid of these aspects. The two thinkers both concern themselves with topics the other ignores. If we define philosophy as cosmological understanding and a perspective on the world that "is concerned with systematic reflection on human life" (Feng 1997), it becomes quite easy to see the difference between Kongzi and Laozi.

Naturalism versus Rule by Virtuosity

Feng Youlan summarizes the differences between Laozi and Kongzi's views well:

> The two most important trends in Chinese thought are Confucianism and Daoism. They represent two opposing extremes of the same axis. . . . Confucianism emphasizes being a responsible citizen, whereas Daoism concentrates on an individual's inner states and innate tendencies. . . .
>
> People often say that Kongzi taught names [that should correspond to reality and behavior], while Laozi and Zhuangzi talked about being 'self-so' [natural]. The relationship between these trends in Chinese thought is roughly equivalent to the relationship between the Classicists and Romantics in Western thought. (1997).

These differences, along with those mentioned above, make up only one aspect of their relationship. Confucianism and Daoism also share many similarities, which is unsurprising since they come from the same tradition. Most notable are the following eight.

1. Both schools believe it is best to hold to the "middle" (*zhong* 中), or avoid extremes.

2. Both also advocate harmony—with others and with nature. This is especially well developed in both the Daoist *Zhuangzi* and Confucian *Mengzi* in the notion of "harmony between heavens and humanity" (*tianren heyi* 天人合一). Both schools believe, for example, that conflicts between persons should be avoided, and that if they do occur, the best outcome is to dissolve them.[1]

3. Theories in both Confucianism and Daoism revolve around an appreciation of the subjective human experience that does not seek to differentiate from or dissect the natural world.

---

[1] Translator's note: As opposed to seeking justice or siding with the "right" party.

4. This also means that neither school talks much about the afterlife, gods, ghosts, or spirits. They focus on human affairs.

5. They both uphold simplicity, naturalness, and sincerity as important character traits or values.

6. Neither sees harsh systems of punishment as effective methods for teaching or governance.

7. They are similarly critical of heavy taxes.

8. Both look to the past for guidance, cherishing the model of a supposed "golden era" at the beginning of human existence.[2]

We see here how Chinese culture with its various worldviews formed during the Western Zhou. Its overarching foundation of humanistic and civic-minded thinking congealed at this time, and the similarities between Kongzi and Laozi give evidence of this fact. Moreover, they were not alone. During the Spring and Autumn period, human reason flourished and a large number of intellectuals debated—all sharing a similar ideological basis.

Zhang Guangzhi notes, "The Xia, Shang, and Zhou dynasties represent a continuous culture, namely Chinese culture, though certain minor discrepancies existed within them" (1983). These "minor discrepancies" were regional, as for example between the Northern and Southern schools of thought,[3] and the distinct cultures of Zou and Lu or Qi and Chu. Cai Yuanpei writes,

> North and south vary greatly in many ways. During the Spring and Autumn period, the state of Chu remained the common enemy of Qi and the Jin states, and eventually was considered barbarous [i.e., not Chinese]. The conflict left its mark not only on politicians; it led scholars with similar social ideologies to set off in opposite directions, as well. Laozi represents the south's critique of northern thought. . . .
>
> Laozi advocated "taking the lower position"—a common position for scholars in the south. His real contributions were in metaphysics, which far surpassed the northern Confucians and built its worldview on an empirical foundation.

---

[2] Translator's note: Whereas Western thinkers are often looking to the future, or afterlife.

[3] Northern thinkers (*beifang zhi xuezhe* 北方之学者) apparently were first distinguished from southern ones in the *Mengzi* in the context of the southerner Chen Liang 陈良, a "product of Chu" (*Chu san* 楚产). North and south, according to Liu Xianmei 刘先枚, were more or less divided by the middle and lower reaches of the Yellow River.

> Southerners criticized northern intellectuals for their complex social customs and complicated institutional systems. They argued that they overlooked the importance of personal cultivation. In general, northerners looked at worldly phenomena and tried to discover rules or patterns, while southerners investigated the cosmos itself, asking much deeper questions (1970)

Here Cai points out that already in the Spring and Autumn period, north and south had their own distinct intellectual atmospheres. At that time, Chu represented the south and Qi the north. Scholars in these states, along with Jin and others, often debated with one another. Their distinct ways of understanding manifest in social and political practices, with Laozi representing the southern scholars' reactionary response to Zhou dynasty customs and institutions.

Such regional distinctions in thought are well recorded in the *Hanshu* 汉书 (History of the Han Dynasty). Here we find "those from the states of Zou and Lu defend studying the classics, while in Qi and Chu they mostly debate ideas." These classifications hold up when drawn along Confucian and Daoist lines. The Confucians place heavy emphasis on studying classics, whereas Laozi and Zhuangzi rarely mention such book learning, focusing rather on individual reflection and empathy. Feng Youlan talks about Laozi "having the spirit of the people of Chu." He writes, "Those from the state of Chu did not enjoy the benefits of Zhou dynasty culture, nor were they bound by its restrictions. They pioneered their own ways of thinking" (1997).

Recently, Ren Jiyu has gone even further in his comparison of Chu philosophy with that of Zou and Lu.

> The characteristic thought of the state of Chu can best be seen in the *Chuci* 楚辞 [Songs of Chu], *Laozi*, and *Zhuangzi*. Thinking in this region mainly centered on questioning the structure and origin of the cosmos and the relationship of humans with nature, and their place therein. This type of inquiry is precisely what thinkers in the Central Plains, in the state of Zhou, disregarded.
>
> Laozi and Zhuangzi seldom mention day-to-day interactions between people or political life; when they do, it is often disdainfully. In Zhou and Lu, scholars carried forward the customs of the Western Zhou. They took Yao, Shun, and Yu as exemplars, and studied the Six Classics. They upheld the patriarchal system to maintain social order and political power. Chu thinkers, on the other hand, were rarely thus fettered by traditional thought. With a special acuteness they boldly criticized the ways of the Western

> Zhou, which proved extremely important for breaking through old institutions and liberating thought. (1979b)

Looking at things historically, we see the rise of Lu under Bo Qin 伯禽—the son of the Duke of Zhou 周公 who ruled from the state's capital at Qufu, Kongzi's hometown—as forming a direct line of political and cultural continuity between Lu and Zhou. The subsequent inheritance of Zhou culture led to the adoption of its repressive patriarchal thinking, which in turn proved a formative influence on Kongzi in his conservative defense of Zhou practices. He dedicated his entire life to "following the ways of Zhou," and tried to convince others to think, act, and govern in those ways.

Laozi, who was also well versed in Zhou culture, conversely approached such practices from the drastically different perspectives characteristic of Chu. He had in fact worked as an imperial librarian-historian, which naturally allowed him to become familiar with many classical texts and artifacts. In addition to his deep knowledge of the ways of the Zhou, he also studied the culture and customs of the earlier Xia dynasty. Wang Bo has written specifically on the relationship between Laozi's thought and Xia culture, which has provided new insights into this aspect of the sources of his thought (1989).

The differences between their schools of thought, distinct regional customs, and individual personalities all led to the divergent approaches of Laozi and Kongzi. These pushed the former to find interest in the relationship between humans and nature, which led him to develop a philosophy of ontology and cosmology. Kongzi's intellectual environment, however, made customs and personal relationships paramount. He therefore focused on social interaction, proposing an ethical theory that he sought to put into practice. In this way, Laozi carried forth a tradition of naturalism while Kongzi advocated the Western Zhou's "rule by virtuosity," each thinker operating within his own strain of culture.

The Importance of Society

Laozi and Kongzi lived during the same time, with Laozi the elder by about twenty years. Kongzi had strong political views as founded on his ethics and sought to make an impact on the world around him. For many years, he went from state to state seeking a ruler who would put his theory into practice, while also meeting with sages or wise men in order to broaden his knowledge. The chapter on Kongzi's disciples in the *Shiji* records, "Kongzi learned from many masters. In Zhou, Laozi taught him; in Wei 卫, Qu Boyu 蘧伯玉; in Qi 齐, Yan Pingzhong 宴平仲; in Chu 楚, Lao Laizi; and in Zheng 郑, Zichan 子产." The *Shiji* biography of Laozi further details Kongzi and Laozi's interactions, supported by Kongzi's acknowledgment of Laozi as his teacher recorded in many pre-Qin texts.

Kongzi famously professed to "transmit and not invent," and the *Lunyu* is widely recognized as the work of his disciples, but the *Laozi* was written by Lao Dan himself. Three major facts support this. First, in terms of theory and worldview, the book is very consistent. The text engages major themes in a clearly structured manner throughout, maintaining uniformity in its overall approach and thought.

Second, the word "I" (*wu* 吾, *wo* 我) appears frequently. Laozi writes, "Few understand me, which makes me valuable;" "My words are easy to understand, and easy to carry out; but no one in the world can understand or carry them out" (ch. 70). This is, of course, Laozi lamenting that his own theory has gone unappreciated by others.

Third, the text contains rhetorical patterns and a regular style, giving expression to a singular voice. For example, the word *xi* 兮 is used throughout the text; the phrase *shiyi* 是以 appears thirty-nine times, and *shiwei* 是谓 is present over twenty times. Idiosyncratic sentence structures like *fuwei* 夫唯 X *shiyi* Y and *shiyi* X *gu* 故 Y are common. The singularity of writing style and its consistency are sufficient to prove that the *Laozi* was composed by a single hand. When we discuss Laozi's ideas, we are able to examine a text he wrote himself, as opposed to Kongzi's thought, which has been transmitted only later, through the words of his disciples.

That both Kongzi and Laozi belonged to the class of scholars (*shi* 士) did not prevent them from harboring different attitudes toward Zhou culture. Fan Wenlan writes, "Kongzi's theory is the crystallization of the thought of the *shi* class." He explains,

> Before scholars went into office, they lived common lives alongside ordinary citizens. They were able to experience the hardships of such living and understood 'being economical and sparing the people [from too much work], and using people at the appropriate times.' . . .
>
> When they applied for government positions, they would appear to their superiors as noblemen with eyes for profit and conservative thinking. When they were poor and disappointed with their careers, they would sympathize with commoners and hold progressive ideas. Such scholars spent most of their time seeking advancement rather than considering the

plights of commoners, so their thinking was more often conservative than progressive, and they were more likely to compromise than dissent. (1949)

Fan's classification is useful for understanding the approaches of Kongzi and Laozi. While both displayed characteristics of the scholar class, the latter's philosophy expressed an exceptional awareness and respect for commoners, whereas Kongzi classified such thinking as belonging to "petty people" (*xiaoren* 小人). In the *Lunyu*, for example, hermits with Daoist-like ideas criticize Kongzi's disciple Zilu for "not using his body to work, and being unable to distinguish the five grains" (18.7). The master himself admits to, and is even proud of, ignoring agricultural knowledge. Later, Fan Chi 樊迟 asks Kongzi about learning to farm, and the master calls him *xiaoren* (13.4).

Laozi, on the contrary, often takes these so-called "petty" people into consideration, writing, "A ruler without virtuosity tithes [farmers]" (ch. 79).[4] Here Laozi sides with commoners, condemning high taxation as too heavy a burden on the people and therefore lacking virtuosity in the ruler, which he views as a major requirement for legitimate rulership. Laozi also writes, "When Dao prevails in the world, fast and strong horses are used for hauling manure" (ch. 46). In other words, if a state is well ordered, has a good ruler and government, then the best horses will all be on farms working rather than on military or other expeditions. Laozi continues, "When war-horses are stationed in borderlands, the world does not accord with Dao" (ch. 46).

Here we see Laozi's opposition to militarism as based on his concern for the wellbeing of common farmers. He bitterly decries the suffering war brings to common people. "Wherever an army is stationed, thorns and briars will grow [i.e., the land will become wild and dangerous]. When there is a great campaign, bad years are sure to follow" (ch. 30). This is Laozi's expression of sympathy for the people, a call for rulers to "align their heart-and-mind with the people's" (ch. 49)

Many scholars have argued that Laozi, as much as Daoism in general, rejects society and advocates eremitism. In reality, Laozi is just as concerned with public life and engaging with the world as Kongzi. The major differences between the two are their views on human culture and the methods of social and political interaction they advocate. Laozi famously declares the way of Dao to involve cultivating and fostering the

---

[4] Translator's note: This is not the standard reading of this line, *wude siche* 无德司彻. The character *che* 彻, here taken to mean "tithes [farmers]," is generally read as "takes extreme measures [for one's own benefit]."

flourishing of the world's myriad beings, but not expropriating them for oneself—a position further reiterated in his advocacy of "not struggling" (ch 4). This is not a doctrine of passivity; on the contrary, it strongly encourages action, rebuking greed and excessive desire for control.

Looking at Laozi contextually, we see that he directs these ideas at the ruling class, insisting that their political power must be used responsibly and not simply to satisfy personal desires. Laozi became a "hidden sage" or hermit in his later years, not to withdraw from the world, but rather as retirement following the success of his career as an official. Even Kongzi, with his relentless passion for implementing his ideas in the world, had a back-up plan of floating away on the high seas.[5] Understanding the challenges of an imperfect world, all thinkers, including Laozi and Kongzi, span the world of ideals and that of practicality, at times engaging with society and at others taking refuge from it.

The two masters further shared concerns regarding the safety and organization of the state. Laozi uses the word "Dao" to describe a well-ordered state, and the sympathetic view he takes toward commoners is reflected in his political advice. Laozi aims to convince leaders to develop policies and plans that accord with the interests of the people. This involves refraining from using excessive force and "unbridled action" (*wangwei* 妄为), that is, acting recklessly, greedily, or outside of one's social role. Laozi uses the terms "self-so" or "natural" and "non-assertive action" to denote the ruler's ideal form of action. His worry is that those in control may be overwhelmed or consumed by their power. Laozi famously writes, "Ordering a large state is like frying a small fish" (ch. 60), encouraging people to focus on minor details and observe harmony.

This differs fundamentally from Kongzi's attitude toward politics, which is assertive and calls for "rule by virtuosity." He expects people to fold under the influence of virtuous rulers. "The exemplary person [*junzi* 君子] has power like the wind; the petty people have the virtuosity of grass. When the wind blows, grass must bend" (*Lunyu* 12.19). When compared to Laozi's understanding of humans' natural state as already in accord with Dao and his advocacy of allowing natural or self-so development, we see quite clearly how deeply the two differ in this regard.

Laozi's ideal for government includes not only concern with a state's peace and stability; it looks at the entire world, i.e., "everything under the heavens (*tianxia* 天下). The depth of this concern is clear from

---

[5] "If *dao* cannot be carried out, will you [Zilu] float away with me on a raft on the high seas?" 道不行 乘槎浮于海 (*Lunyu* 5.7)

the frequency with which he uses the term—sixty-one times across twenty-nine chapters—as well as its variety of contexts.

Laozi envisions the ideal state as small in area and population. He believes that this is more conducive to carrying out his political theory, even though relations with larger states may be tricky. As he says,

> Large states acquire [benefits from] smaller states by acquiescing to them.
> Small states acquire [benefits from] larger states by acquiescing to them.
> Large states only wish to nourish their growing population.
> Small states only wish to have good relations and serve their people.
> [If they work together] both parties get what they want,
> As long as the large state is humble. (ch. 61)

Tu Youguang further explicates the cooperation required for their harmonious interaction. "The large state must be humble of its own accord; then other states, regardless of size, will unite with it. . . . In reality, the only way to maintain a small state is if it allows itself to be directed by a larger state" (1995).

Finally, Laozi advocates "honoring the world as if it was one's own body" (ch. 13), and outlines specific steps for doing so, beginning with the body and working outward to family, community, state, and world (ch. 55). Later this served as the blueprint for the analogous Confucian idea. As Tu says, "The Confucian work, "Great Learning" [*Daxue* 大学], states, 'From the Emperor to the common people, the cultivation of the body is most essential for all.' While this teaching was indeed developed by Kongzi, Mengzi, and Xunzi, the *Laozi* clearly influenced them" (1995).The fundamental thinking behind this Confucian concept came from Laozi.

Heavens, Dao, and Virtuosity

Feng Youlan argues that the word for "heavens" has five main connotations. It can be used to describe the sky, a heavenly god or other will, heavenly fate or teleology, a natural heaven, and heavenly ethics or morality (1986).

Laozi's idea of the heavens refers to the entire universe as organized naturally or self-so. For humans, the best or most efficacious acts follow what is natural, the natural organization of the heavens. Kongzi, on the other hand, sees the heavens as sacred. He develops morality and rites in an attempt to encourage people to cultivate themselves accordingly. These two distinct views on human action are founded on different conceptions of the heavens.

The concept the heavens was probably first formed sometime around the shift from the Shang to the Zhou (Li 1980), and Laozi's use of the term can be traced back to the *Yijing*, *Shijing*, and *Shangshu*. In these texts, the heavens often simply indicate the sky of the natural world. This concept, further developed by Zhuangzi, later became an essential foundation for Chinese atheistic thought.

Kongzi's conception of the heavens inherits the Western Zhou's orthodox view of the "heavenly mandate" or "destiny" (*tianming* 天命). He may also have found and developed various less secular versions as seen in the *Shijing* and *Shangshu*. In the *Lunyu*, the term "heavens" appears sixteen times, mostly pointing to a conscious or teleological entity. Kongzi remarks, for example, "Offending the heavens leaves nothing to pray to" (3.13), and "Life and death are fated, [the distribution of] wealth and rank is [written] in the heavens" (12.5). Many of Kongzi's contemporaries held similar views in which they saw the heavens as having divine powers. Kongzi takes this further, directly connecting the heavens to people's lives (12.5).

The *Lunyu*, however, includes one major exception to this vision. It records the master as having said, "Do the heavens speak? The four seasons rotate. Beings are born. Do the heavens speak?" (17.19). Here Kongzi points out that the change of seasons and the birth of beings are not controlled by the will of the heavens; rather, they occur naturally. Feng Youlan comments on this line, saying that the heavens "govern through non-assertive action" (1997). This is the same term Laozi uses to describe great rulers. Feng's terminology here ought to be seen, therefore, as in reference to Laozi's influence on Kongzi.

Laozi's view of the heavens rejects the more traditional elements that Kongzi developed and emphasizes their qualities. Laozi replaces the concept of the heavenly mandate with that of "return to destiny" (*fuming* 復命), a cyclical conception of natural, self-so development as reflected in the heavens and throughout the natural world. It involves developing to an extreme and then returning to an original state. "Going back to the roots is stillness; this is called return to destiny. Return to destiny is constant" (ch. 16).

Such development arises from the nature of beings, and therefore Laozi calls for the absence of interference with natural processes. All beings are born and grow before eventually returning to their root—a quiet state of tranquility. From this latter state, beings become pregnant, both literally and metaphorically, with the seeds of new life and action, and this is "return to destiny," best understood as similar to the inevitable completion of lifecycles. There are many possible interpretations of this pattern. We can explain it as returning to nature, the root, or to a genuine state. It can also refer to a renewal of impetus, power, or life.

The *Zuozhuan*, which preceded the *Laozi*, explains "mandate" as the life all beings are given, nourished by the vital energy or life force (*qi* 气) between the heavens and the earth.[6] Laozi's concept closely relates to this.

Kongzi, on the other hand, uses the term to indicate something closer to destiny, matching more traditional religious interpretations. In fact, he often uses the term in connection with his quasi-divine understanding of the heavens and emphasizes its importance. "The exemplary person reveres three things: the heavenly mandate, great people, and the words of sages" (*Lunyu* 16.8). Note the order here, putting the heavenly mandate first, immediately preceding "great people."

Kongzi highlights both the importance of the mandate and its relationship with great rulers, establishing a basis for the idea that political power comes from the divine. He believes that only exemplary persons respect the heavenly mandate, and that common people are unaware of it and therefore lack respect for it as well as for their rulers and great people. Following the above, the *Lunyu* says explicitly, "Petty people do not know or respect the heavenly mandate; they lack respect for great people." Taken as a whole, the passage shows that knowing the heavenly mandate is a way of differentiating social status or class. In Kongzi's views, his traditional beliefs and conservative politics clearly shine through.

Broadly speaking, Dao in the *Laozi* is metaphysical and cosmological, whereas in the *Lunyu* it is ethical and concerned with human relations. Kongzi rarely mentions the heavenly or cosmological Dao (*tiandao*) that Laozi discusses so often.

---

[6] *Zuozhuan*, Chenggong 30 has Liu Kang 刘康 say: "The life given to people between the heavens and the earth is called 'mandate'." Yang Baijun 杨柏峻 glosses, "The Ancients believed there was a neutral *qi* between the heavens and the earth giving people life. *Ming* means life."

Heavenly Dao

"Heavenly Dao" is a much later term than the heavens or destiny. Early records show it as governing people's fortunes, based on a sort of karmic principle. The *Guoyu* reports, "The first kings said 'The heavenly Dao rewards the good and punishes the bad'" (1.21).

Records from the early Spring and Autumn period, however, show the concept referring to the regular movement of heavenly bodies, (*Zuozhuan* 3.4), and by the end of the period this had become common. The *Guoyu* records Laozi's contemporary Fan Li as saying,

> When the heavenly Dao is full, it does not overflow. When prosperous, it is not arrogant. When it accomplishes things, it does not tout its achievements. . . .
>
> The heavenly Dao is brilliant, and sun and moon take it as constant [as they move]. They take the heavenly Dao as their model whether shining or dim. When yang reaches its utmost, it becomes yin; when yin reaches its utmost, it becomes yang. The sun rises but it also sets. The moon becomes full but it also wanes. (8.7)

Fan Li rids the notion of the heavenly Dao of abstruse religious concepts and superstition, focusing instead on yin-yang ideology and a concept of cyclic development very similar to Laozi's return to destiny. Fan Li's intent is to deduce natural laws of transformation and apply them to humans, which serves to warn people against arrogance and conceit—all perfectly in line with Laozi.

In Laozi's theory, human relations and politics take the heavenly Dao's natural order as their model. According to Laozi, successful persons should avoid fame (ch. 9), people should seek benefit without harming others (ch. 81), and virtuosity or success should be achieved without struggling (ch. 72). These suggestions and the model of the heavenly Dao are based on arise from Laozi's moral indignation over his disappointment with society. The heavenly Dao's balancing power pushes against social injustices, especially the use of power for personal gain and extortion. Calling for a redistribution of wealth and restructuring of social order, he writes, "The heavenly Dao diminishes overabundance and supplements deficiency" (ch. 72). Clearly, Laozi's cosmology and social outlook are closely intertwined.

Lu Yusan argues, "Laozi's view of the heavenly Dao contains three important elements. First, full and empty transform into one another.

Second, all beings follow a cyclical pattern, progressing and returning. Third, the heavens, the earth, and humans can be in harmony as long as they all follow the rules of such transformation and cyclicality" (1987). In fact, this understanding of the heavenly Dao greatly informs Laozi's further development of his concept of Dao.

Laozi was the first person in history to formulate a systematic theory of Dao. Indeed, he built an entire philosophy centering on it. Dao is the origin of all beings as well as the pattern, by which they continually transform. Laozi specifically describes Dao as transforming from a state of having form to a state of formlessness, using "nonbeing" or "nonpresence" (*wu* 无) and "being" or "presence" (*you* 有) to discuss this process. Nonbeing also refers to the limitlessness of Dao and to its expansion to extremes, while being denotes its fullness—its being all beings and governance of them. Its pervasiveness—the fact that it *is* everything—is part and parcel of the idea of Dao governing these same things.

Laozi strongly emphasizes Dao's natural and non-assertive tendencies. He writes, "Humans follow the earth, the earth follows the heavens, the heavens follow Dao, and Dao follows nature [self-so]" (ch. 25). In other words, Laozi thinks that the heavens, earth, and humans all follow the natural patterns of Dao. Traditional religious beliefs see a god or other metaphysical entity as the creator and controller of the world. However, Laozi's proclamation that "Dao follows nature" rejects anything supernatural or divine. His assertion that "Dao is consistent in not acting [assertively], and there is nothing that is not done" (ch. 37) expresses that Dao simply follows what is natural, as all beings should. When there is no interference with natural states, beings flourish. Upsetting this only hinders development and order in the world.

Laozi also very clearly describes Dao's course as cyclical. When he writes "return is the movement of Dao" (ch. 40), he means that all beings develop toward their opposites, return to their original state, and are continually reborn to restart the process. This holds true of individual beings and events as well as the cosmos itself.

Discussing the origin of the cosmos, Laozi says, "Dao generates one, one generates two, two generates three, and three generates all beings. Everything carries yin and embraces yang. These energies clash and are harmonized" (ch. 42). Here one, two, and three detail the process by which Dao generates all beings. Originally, Dao is an undifferentiated mass (*hundun* 混沌) and everything combined as one. When the mass splits into yin and yang, they begin to clash with one another and harmonize into distinct entities. This interaction makes up the foundation of all beings.

Laozi built a cosmology completely absent of a god with a specific intention or design, which was of tremendous groundbreaking significance in the history of philosophy, but inverts the relationship between Dao and the manifest world. This vision greatly impacted the thought of the Jixia Academy, Zhuangzi, and the *Yizhuan* 易传 (Commentary on the Changes). The Jixia Academy saw Dao as original, primordial vital energy and developed that concept toward materialism. Zhuangzi engages the comprehensiveness of Dao on an epistemological level, and claims Dao to be the highest realm of human life. The *Yizhuan* says, "one [time] yin and one [time] yang, this is Dao," borrowing from the *Laozi* to engage a concept of dichotomy.

Kongzi on Dao

Kongzi holds Dao in equally high regard, although he understands it in a fundamentally different manner. Unlike Laozi, he has little interest in Dao's metaphysical or cosmological aspects. For him, Dao is ethical and political. The word "Dao" appears seventy-seven times in the *Lunyu*, and refers to morality almost every time. Accordingly, the heavenly Dao appears only once, when Kongzi's disciple Zigong says, "The Master's discussion of innate tendencies (*xing* 性) and the heavenly Dao are not to be heard" (5.13). Zhu Xi glosses this, "The Master did not remark on innate tendencies and the heavenly Dao." This clearly shows that Kongzi established only a weak (if any) understanding of the heavenly Dao.

One of the most famous passages in the *Lunyu* is "Kongzi said, 'My Dao [teaching] is all-pervasive and one [unified theory]'" (4.15). His Dao is not an abstract entity or pattern, but rather a standardized ethics of human relations and rites based on the patriarchal and feudal systems of his time. Throughout the *Lunyu*, he reveres a vision of the past when "counties had Dao" and grieves the loss of Dao in modern society. In one passage, Youzi 有子 says, "The ancient kings' Dao was most magnificent," (1.12). Another records Kongzi as saying, "The world has been without Dao for a long time now" (3.24).

Kongzi laments the fall of the Zhou, when Dao prevailed, and takes Zhou rites as the basis for his Dao. He believes that rulers should follow Dao, defined as Zhou culture and rites, that ministers should treat their superiors in accordance with it. He says one should be "in line with Dao when one serves one's leader" (*Lunyu* 11.24). Youzi also explains the fundamentality of filial reverence and brotherly love, and that those who have cultivated these are unlikely to offend their superiors. Such a claim is clearly ethically charged, which turns the generation of Dao into a moral event. However, what has made Kongzi's theory so appealing to rulers throughout the ages is not necessarily this focus on ethical practices, but the compliance suggested by it. The *Lunyu* records, "Ziyou 子游 said to the Master, 'I have heard you say that petty people who study Dao are easily ruled" (17.4).

Dao is thus central to the thought of both Laozi and Kongzi, but their understanding of this concept differs, resulting in two unique perspectives on the world. Of almost equal importance to both masters is the concept of virtuosity (*de* 德),[7] and they have very different interpretations of the term. For Laozi, it means "grasping Dao." The *Guanzi* equates "virtuosity" with its homophone *de* 得, which means "grasp," "achieve," or "arrive" (36.6). Zhuangzi writes, "Beings acquiring their own generation—that is 'virtuosity'" (12.8). These passages are inspired by the *Laozi*,

> Beings are produced by Dao and nourished by virtuosity.
> The material world determines their form,
> Completed by their circumstances.
> Of them, none does not honor Dao and value virtuosity.
> Honoring Dao and valuing virtuosity is not destiny.
> It is the innate tendency of all beings. (ch. 51)

Dao and virtuosity command the reverence of all beings, because they generate and develop through them. Dao produces all beings and is their essence; virtuosity is their part that grasps Dao. Dao is at once abstract and concrete.

Zhuangzi inherited this notion from Laozi, and elaborated on it. The "Dechongfu" 德充符 chapter of the *Zhuangzi* (ch. 5) is nothing but a lengthy discussion of virtuosity. Importantly, nothing in this chapter suggests that virtuosity has any ethical implications. Those who have experience in the world and know the origin and entirety of the cosmos have virtuosity. They are "great ancestral masters" (*dazongshi* 大宗师, also the title of *Zhuangzi*, ch. 6)—people who embody Dao and are full of virtuosity. Zhuangzi's cosmos is a great vitality of continuous renewal

---

[7] Translator's note: "Virtuosity" translates *de*, a term that has proven highly contentious. Other major translations include "virtue," "virtuousness," "ethics," "power," and "to grasp."

and growth. Zhuangzi sees the entirety of this as "Dao," and virtuosity as the vitality of worldly phenomena.

Returning to Kongzi, we find that in his thought neither Dao nor virtuosity has the same kind of rich philosophical meaning that Laozi and Zhuangzi see. Like his concept of Dao, Kongzi's virtuosity is entirely concerned with culture, rites, and ethics in human society. The *Lunyu* notes, "Kongzi said: 'Dao [teachings) should be in line with [social] virtues and uniformity should be in line with the rites; then people will have a sense of shame, and moreover become proper" (2.3). Here virtuosity and rites benefit one another. Virtuosity means to act in accordance with Zhou culture.

Dao and virtuosity are also defined in terms of the patriarchal system of China during Kongzi's time. The *Lunyu* records, "Kongzi said: 'If someone acts according to their father's Dao [teaching] for three years after his death, then they may be called filial" (1.11). The connection between Dao and ethics is obvious here. The same chapter also says, "Zengzi said: 'If people are attentive to their own mortality, and live up to past models, they will naturally become more virtuous'" (1.9).

Again, the connection between virtuosity and ethics, based on a patriarchal society, is evident. When people follow their father's Dao, their own virtuosity (i.e., morality) strengthens. In Kongzi's world, people require positive examples to serve as models for their own actions. In the family this should be the father, and in society the ruler. Kongzi's visions of Dao and virtuosity form a world in which "When the wind [of a ruler] blows, grass [petty people] must bend" (12.19). Dao allows the populace to be ruled effectively. For Kongzi, there is no real tendency for order or harmony in the world unless people cultivate it within themselves through a strict cultural system of rites. He understands both Dao and virtuosity within the bounds of Zhou institutions.

Human Innate Tendencies

From ontology to the origin of the cosmos, Dao's foundational role in Laozi's philosophy works alongside another concept, the innate tendencies (*xing* 性) of all beings. This dynamic roots in the relationship between Laozi's conceptions of Dao and self-so (*ziran*)—a term generally translated as nature, but which in the *Laozi* can often be more accurately understood as "according to a thing itself." Self-so is in fact Dao's own basic innate tendency.

Dao's self-so tendency means that beings are generated without intent or purpose. Dao gives the objects of the world no external orders or set goals besides following what is self-so for each—their own innate tendencies. Laozi's praise of Dao as "nurturing without controlling" stands in sharp contrast to the creator gods of Western religions, especially Christianity. After Jehovah created the universe, he made certain that people followed his word. Even the slightest offenses were punished, and when his will was not followed, he flooded to world to start over. Laozi's Dao, in contrast, follows the principle of non-assertive action, which aligns its operations with those of individual beings that make up the world (Hu 1989). As Dao makes up the beings of the world, one also finds its characteristics in them—an ontological theory that profoundly affected Zhuangzi's philosophy.

The *Zhuangzi* understands beings as created spontaneously according to their own unique conditions. When the "Tianzifang" chapter (ch. 21) speaks of "the supreme height of the sky, supreme thickness of the earth, and supreme luminosity of the sun and moon," it is reminiscent of the fact that these are intrinsic characteristics or natures of these entities, suggesting that all beings have their own individual tendencies. The "Tiandao" chapter (ch. 13) similarly notes, "The sky and earth maintain constancy; the sun and moon maintain brightness; stars maintain their course; animals maintain affinity for their own kind; plants hold their place." Again, we find that each being or species has its own way of existing. The word "maintain" (*gu* 固) shows that these are original rather than developed states of each entity—their natural conditions, uninfluenced by outside factors. The "Qiwulun" 齐物论 chapter (ch. 2), moreover, contains a series of discussions about the equality of different beings and perspectives. "The wind blows on all beings producing myriad sounds, yet each resonates and ceases of its own." The *Zhuangzi* insists that even when the innumerable noises of the world sound together, each being retains its own voice.

Laozi's theory of individual natural tendencies has also influenced Confucian thought. For example, the idea that there is a constant natural tendency throughout the cosmos unbound to destiny (*mo zhi ming* 莫之命) occurs also in the *Mengzi*. "That which does not act yet gets things done is the heavens" (5.6). The idea that the heavens "do not act" (*mo zhi wei* 莫之为) mirrors Laozi's rejection of higher destiny in the world.

Based on the idea of all beings having individual natures, Laozi advocates "helping beings develop according to their own paths [i.e., self-so]" (ch. 64) in order to create conditions where "all beings change spontaneously/of themselves [*zihua* 自化]. . . [and] everything in the world aligns itself properly [*ziding* 自定]" (ch. 37). Laozi, indeed, is quite outspoken in his belief that the world naturally orders itself in the absence of interference, stating, "Without human control, natural evenness [or harmony] occurs" (ch. 32)

Laozi sums up his view, highlighting its implications for governance, as "I act non-assertively, and the people transform themselves; I love stillness, and the people correct themselves; I do not manage beings, and the people become rich themselves; I am free of desires, and the people become simple themselves" (ch. 57). Like similar texts of the period, Laozi's "I" identifies with a ruler, and is therefore expounding on all that can be achieved by rulers through refraining from selfish and excessive interference in the matters of one's subjects. Such restraint allows the people to educate, cultivate, and develop themselves. In Laozi's view, this will happen naturally, requiring only that the populace is allow to remain in keeping with their own dispositions, and thereby the cosmos.

Laozi's emphasis on natural tendencies and self-governance arose in reaction to common problems during the Spring and Autumn period, when rampant militarism, deception, thievery, and coercion devastated the lives of common people. The brutal clashes between states in particular edified Laozi's anti-war stance. Many rulers also set high taxes resulting in famine, leading Laozi to criticize leaders for their greed. Perhaps the biggest issue he had with his society, however, was the extravagant luxury of the nobility. Laozi argues, "If rare items are not highly valued, the people will not become thieves" (ch. 3). He further proclaims that people should "do away with contriving for riches," and that "The more restrictions there are in the world, the more impoverished the people. . . . The more laws and decrees are displayed, the more robbers there will be" (ch. 57). All of these aspects of Laozi's thought clearly reflect the social conditions of his times.

Learning and Education

With such an emphasis on noninterference with natural tendencies, it comes as no surprise that the *Laozi* famously criticizes education, "Get rid of learning and there will be no worries" (ch. 19). While this line was certainly directed at what Laozi saw as the triviality and tediousness of

Spring and Autumn period scholars, it also, like much of Laozi's theory, follows a spirit already established in earlier texts. By Laozi's time, many thinkers already agreed that there was "nothing harmful about ignoring education" (*wuxue buhai* 无学不害). A passage in the *Zuozhuan*, for example, challenges the value of learning when an official attending an imperial funeral in Zhou talks to Yuan Bolu 原伯鲁 and discovers the great minister "does not enjoy learning" (*bu yuexue* 不悦学). Laozi would have been familiar with this passage and other scholars who shared this view.

We should, however, note that the type of study or education Laozi opposes is directed toward specific targets: political theory, rites, music, and studies associated with governmental work. (This is how contemporaries of Laozi such as Kongzi, Mengzi, and Xunzi speak of education.) The *Laozi* presents a perspective wary of power politics, and therefore of "official education" (*guanxue* 官学), which made it a pioneer of "private education" in China. Texts written before the *Laozi* concentrate on history, politics (including war), or culture (e.g., rites and music), and are intended to aid anyone seeking office or already in government. The *Laozi*, though politically rich, has much to say about the individual and goes far beyond advice for acting morally or otherwise impressing officials.

This strain of thought runs contrary to the Confucian project. The three major pre-Qin Confucian scholars speak with one voice about the importance of education. Kongzi says, "Without learning rites it is impossible for one to be established" (16.13). Being "established" (*li* 立) for him means becoming a moral person who through study understands how to live according to proper customs. In other words, education and rites combine to command appropriate behavior. Kongzi further remarks, "The exemplary person studies extensively, and is restrained by rites" (6.27).

Mengzi defines study or education (*xue* 学) as "everything that makes morality understandable" (3A.3). He, too, believes that without education people cannot possibly be ethical. Xunzi's comment on education is the most informative because he indirectly defines rites, as well. He writes, "Studying rites is the utmost [of education], and it ends there" (1.12). He inherits a great deal from the *Lunyu* and *Mengzi*. The coupling of education and morality was, as we have seen, well established. Xunzi's comment equates rites with the highest level of study, an identification of morality that expresses the importance and dominance of the rites in all aspects of life.

This is why Laozi rejects education. He is skeptical about the ability of political and rites thought to affect our innate dispositions positively, most importantly believing that they restrict our natural inclinations. Confucians define almost every part of human life in terms of rites, and when they specify propriety and impropriety, they are actually looking to control activities that extend beyond public life and politics. Laozi thinks that people will be better off without these limitations.

The Rites

Laozi directly attacks the rites, saying, "shallowness of loyalty and sincerity makes [rites] the beginnings of disorder. . . . The great man resides in what is thick [genuine], and not what is thin [superficial]. [The great man] resides in the fruit [actuality], not the flower [appearances]" (ch. 38) The *Laozi* then presents four major reasons for this harsh view of rites.

1. As Hou Wailu points, Laozi sees the rites as "a sign of the old systems of aristocratic and authoritative dictatorship, which distinguishes sharply between aristocrat and commoner, honorable and inferior, and those in higher and lower positions" (Hou, Zhao, and Du 1957: 15) These distinctions, rooted in social class, are also reflected in the moral sphere. Laozi straightforwardly challenges these appraisals with his statement "The honorable are rooted in the inferior; the high have their foundation in the low" (ch. 39). He seeks to upset aristocratic values by noting the interconnectedness of the social classes, particularly the nobility's reliance on lower social strata.

2. Laozi sees the rites as unnecessary and overly elaborate formalities, their real function to restrain and limit people's heart-and-mind (*xin* 心).

3. Laozi believes that rulers purposely moralize the rites to usurp power and control people. The *Zhuangzi* intensifies this argument in its "Quqie" 胠篋 chapter (ch. 10).

4. The final and perhaps largest problem is that rites and the morality equated with them violate nature and natural human inclination. Nietzsche summarizes Laozi's view when he states that all traditional ethical systems have been so foolish and contrary to nature that humanity would have perished from every one had it gained full power (Nietzsche 2001: 28-8). This is close to Laozi's point, when he decries those attempting to establish ritual systems as "the superficial appearance of Dao and origin of stupidity" (ch. 38).

Laozi's radical rejection of the rites represents a passionately progressive position that has developed and undergone various reforms in Chinese history. Kongzi and his followers represent the opposite extreme—a conservative approach to the rites and the importance of culture. From these two stances, we see elements of Daoism and Confucianism's later development into representative schools of "official" and "popular" philosophy.

The rites being central to Kongzi's thought is what pushed him to focus so intently on keeping the culture and institutions of the Zhou alive. Fan Wenyuan argues that before Mengzi, "Confucianism was actually just the study of rites" (1954). Hou Wailu notes, "'Establishing oneself through the rites' (*li yu li* 立于礼) is the center of Kongzi's thought. . . . Kongzi's view of history is really just commentary on whether the rites were properly implemented or not" (1998). He further comments, "For Kongzi, rites is the standard for organization and order in the world. . . . His criticism of music and rites in the Spring and Autumn period was not a rejection of old ways based on new understanding. On the contrary, Kongzi wanted to follow the old ways in rectifying existing understanding. He seeks to 'correct reality so that it corresponds to names [titles]' [*xunming yi qiushi* 循名以求实]" (Hou, Zhao, and Du 1957: 141-2). Gao Heng supports this:

> Kongzi emphasizes rites in politics as an effective method for establishing order. . . . He expects rulers to harmonize the people with rites and the people to respect rites. Pre-Qin scholars use the word "rites" to describe two types of institution: first, social establishments and customs, including everything from taxes to the characterization of and relationships between the different classes; second, ceremonies comprised of weddings, funerals, mourning, archery, the court formality, and so on. Kongzi extends these meanings even further, placing great importance on maintaining feudal order, patriarchal hereditary systems, and other institutions that promote class distinction. . . .
>
> These traditional organizations ensured that aristocrats enjoyed all kinds of special privileges and power in society. Kongzi bestowed affirmation on this. [When asked what the first thing he would do if in power,] Kongzi says, '[I would make sure] leaders lead, ministers minister, fathers father and sons son' [12.11]. He opposes 'the Ji family using eight rows of dancers' [3.1] [usurping a royal prerogative] and 'the three families using Yong songs' [3.2] [inappropriate for the situation].
>
> Kongzi also cites the *Chunqiu,* saying, 'A corrupt official is a thief,' and strictly observes the distinction of titles and class. This is all so that he can protect hierarchical hereditary institutions. (1963)

Kongzi famously opposed the state of Jin's 晋 *Zhuxing shu* 铸刑书 (Book of Punishments), a "public" set of statutes cast on a metal vessel, placed next to the throne, that symbolically replaced feudal royalty. Kongzi dissented on the basis that publicly standardized laws would disrupt class order, the hierarchy essential to success in governance. The *Zuozhuan* records Kongzi explaining, "With the [rules for] the common people on the vessel [next to the throne], how will they continue to respect the aristocracy? What occupation does the aristocracy have to protect [without the old hereditary system]?" (10.29). Kongzi sees "respect for aristocracy" as part of protecting rites and political order.

Earlier tradition, found in the *Chunqiu*, had already established the use of the rites in constraining both rulers and the people, endorsing their ability to "establish hierarchical positions in society" (*Zuozhuan* 5.2). This way, "Rites are used for ordering the people" (3.2). Accordingly, "rites form government, and government sets the people right" (2.2). These passages express the power the rites have in governing the people.

Kongzi's continue this line of thinking. He says, "[If] rulers and ministers love rites, the people will not dare disrespect them [that is, their government and the rites that it implements]" (13.4). "[If] rulers and ministers love rites, the people will be easy to govern" (14.41). In line with this, the *Liji* comments, "Rites are a ruler's most powerful handle [for governing]" (9.12), an idea that leads Kongzi to support "serving rulers and respecting rites" (15.38).

Kongzi further attacks any violation of the rites, even seemingly trifling matters, such as the examples given above of misused dancing patterns or music, which he views as potentially disastrous. These instances of disloyal conduct, whether small or large, disrupt the proper relationships between names and reality. Kongzi advocates "the proper use of names and titles" (*zhengming* 正名) as a key element in his political theory. The scope of this extends to appropriate differentiation between social classes, and forms part of Kongzi's quest to "restore the rites" (*fuli* 复礼)—that is, systematically revive the former Zhou culture of ritual propriety.

Within this quest to restore the rites, Kongzi strives to engage the more restrictive aspects of rites. In a relatively extreme passage he says that one should not look, listen, speak or act in anyway that is not ritually appropriate (*Lunyu* 12.1). Every aspect of a person's life should accord with the rites: this keeps society under control. Critically, then, the rites prevent the people from rebelling and uphold existing institutions and the power of the ruling classes. Xiao Gongquan 萧公权 understands this aspect of Kongzi's attempt to reinstate Zhou culture well. "Kongzi's attitude toward political rule advocates the people following Zhou customs, which is a conservative political stance. This is likely a major reason for the importance later Confucians attached to absolute rulership" (Xiao and Li 2005)

Humaneness and Responsibility

Many scholars have supposed that Laozi is an anti-moralist or unethical because he proposes to "get rid of humaneness and responsibility" (ch. 19). The full line, however, is: "Get rid of humaneness and responsibility, and the people become filial and kind." Laozi wants people to return to their natural state, which involves them being filial and kind. This is not an anti-moralist approach. Laozi rejects these classic Confucian virtues because, as Wang Xiaobo puts it, "Humaneness and responsibility are values that uphold the patriarchal feudal system, which was the old social structure leftover from the Western Zhou" (1984)

Indeed, the use of these virtues, particularly together, was by no means pioneered by Kongzi or Mengzi; rather, these two drew from a long-standing tradition. The *Shiji* declares, "Humaneness and responsibility make a king" (4.66), and the *Guoyu* delimits the terms: "Exposing dispute and benefiting other peoples, this is not responsibility. Estrangement from one's kin and forming relations with barbarians, this is not ritual propriety. Repaying virtuosity with enmity, this is not humaneness" (1.15). We thus find association between humaneness, responsibility, and the rites long before Laozi and Kongzi, the various virtues already vigorously promoted. Other passages from the *Guoyu* and *Zuozhuan* further clarify this pre-Confucian relationship. When Laozi calls for getting rid of humaneness and responsibility, he does not reject morality, but the established relationship between humaneness, responsibility, rites, and the idea of moral governance. Laozi opposes humaneness and responsibility because they make up a moral code, which props up a ruling class he believes interferes with nature.

Laozi's negative view of humaneness, responsibility, and rites does not, however, extend to morality in general. He rejects orthodox and hypocritical values to make room for an ethical theory based on natural human tendencies. From Laozi's attack on rites for its superficiality (ch. 38), we see the value he attaches to sincerity. In fact, his problem with superficiality is precisely that it stifles sincerity. Laozi remains, like Kongzi, very much concerned with human interactions; however, he wants people to have honest and loyal relations, and he finds pre-established rites disruptive to this.

Historically, "loyalty" or "devotion" (*zhong* 忠), an important aspect in the common binome "trustworthy and loyal" or "faithful and honest" (*zhongxin* 忠信) has two major connotations. It can mean, "benefiting the people," as where the *Zuozhuan* records, "Dao is what is loyal to the people. . . . When rulers think of benefiting the people, that is loyalty" (2.2). Like many virtues, however, it is reciprocal, and therefore can also mean benefiting the rulers. As the *Zuozhuan* notes, "Everyone tries their utmost to be loyal, and would die for the ruler" (7.2). For Laozi the first meaning is more important, whereas Kongzi concentrates on the latter.

Laozi also greatly values trustworthiness, commenting:

> Words are excellent through their trustworthiness. (ch. 8)
> When [rulers] are not trustworthy, [the people] are not trustworthy. (ch. 17)
> I am trustworthy with those who are trustworthy, and I am trustworthy with those who are not trustworthy. Sincerity is trustworthiness. (ch. 49)
> Those who make promises too easily are seldom trustworthy. (ch. 63)
> Trustworthy words are not beautiful, and beautiful words are not trustworthy. (ch. 81)

Laozi's view on morality extends beyond sincerity or trustworthiness, of course. He also explains the importance of "three treasures I am sure to maintain. The first is kindness [*ci*], the second frugality [*jian*] and the third never daring to put myself first in the world [*bugan wei tianxia xian* 不敢为天先]" (ch. 67). The third treasure expresses Laozi's moral principle of not struggling, the scope of which encompasses modesty in its many forms. Laozi's second treasure likewise belongs to his moral understanding. Being frugal means knowing when to be satisfied, acting selflessly and keeping oneself simple and in line with natural patterns.

The first treasure, kindness, can be seen in Laozi's disapproval of war: "Even the best weapons are inauspicious beings, abhorrent to all. Those who know Dao do not use them. . . . If compelled to use them, one should do so prudently and impassionedly" (ch. 31). Another more proactive element of Laozi's conception of kindness appears here, "The sage is good at [*shan* 善][8] saving [i.e. making the most of] people, and therefore never abandons people, and is good at saving beings, and therefore never abandons beings. . . . The kind [*shan*] person is the master of those who are not kind. Those who are not kind are instructive for those who are kind [by serving as negative examples]" (ch. 27).

Kongzi 's Take

Kongzi clearly borrows from Laozi's moral theory in two places. He elaborates on his "repaying enmity with kindness/virtuosity" (ch. 14) and says, "Teaching in a lenient and gentle manner, and not retaliating against actions that are out of line, this is the virtuosity of the South [i.e., Laozi]"(*Liji*, "Zhongyong"). This passage emphasizes the humanistic nature of Laozi's ideas. Laozi's emphasis on non-assertive action and benefiting oneself without harming others is based on a selfless moral understanding. Laozi writes, "The sage does not accumulate things [for himself]. The sage acts for others, and is thereby provided for himself" (ch. 81). Here, Laozi's moral theory sounds similar to Nietzsche's "gift-giving virtuosity" and Erich Fromm's appreciation of giving.

The major difference between Kongzi and Laozi on moral values is the emphasis Kongzi places on the rites. As shown above, Laozi's understanding of kindness shares tremendous qualities of human compassion with Kongzi's humaneness. Unfortunately, Kongzi binds his notion of humaneness in the constraints of the rites in his mission to preserve earlier conservative thinking about politics and morality.

Humaneness and other moral concepts were in popular circulation during the Spring and Autumn period, the word "humane" appearing fifty-seven times in the *Zuozhuan* and twenty-four times in the *Guoyu*. Kongzi's theory, moreover, inherited these ideas and in its roots goes back to various earlier texts. Several major points further elucidate this point.

1. The idea of filial piety, related to humaneness, can be found in the *Shangshu*, where Duke Dan of Zhou 周公旦 says in prayer, "We are humane and filial" (4.8).[9] Feng Youlan argues that humaneness in this

---

[8] Translator's note: The use of *shan* in this passage from the *Laozi* is especially interesting, as invokes both of the character's two major meanings, "to be good at" and "kind," and seems to be drawing on or even highlighting an implicit connection between them.

[9] The word is *kao* 考 ("examine," "check"), but may mean *xiao* 孝 (filiality).

sentence means "following the will of one's ancestors" (1986). The *Zuozhuan* similarly defines humaneness similarly as "not betraying the root," (8.2), and the *Guoyu* records, "Those who are humane love their relatives" (6.8). These similar understandings of humaneness all supported the Zhou dynasty's patriarchal clan system. Kongzi continues this tradition when the *Lunyu* records, "Are not filial and fraternal reverence the root of humaneness?" (1.2). Mengzi also follows this, claiming, "Affection for one's relatives, that is humaneness" (6B 23). Here we find that both of the great Confucian masters teach a conception of humaneness based on their culture's traditional patriarchal clan system.

2. Humaneness can mean "loving people." Although Kongzi is famous for expanding the filial aspect of humaneness to a love for all people, this had already been done in the *Guoyu*, where Xiang Gong 襄公 says, "Love people and one can be humane" (3.26). When Fan Chi asks Kongzi about humaneness, the master replies, "Those who are humane love people" (12.22), clearly echoing Xiang Gong's words.

3. The idea of preferring humaneness or morality above even one's life is also attributed to Kongzi. He says, "The resolute scholar or humaneness person will not preserve life at the expense of harming their humaneness [i.e., virtuosity] and would even sacrifice their life to be humaneness" (15.9). However, the *Guoyu* again had already recorded this idea: "Sacrificing one's life to fulfill one's aspirations, that is humaneness" (8.10).

4. The connection between humaneness and benefiting the state, central to Kongzi's criticism of Guan Zhong (*Lunyu* 3.22) again comes from the *Guoyu*. According to the *Guoyu*, "A humaneness person has [political] achievements" (4.9) and "Benefitting the country, that is what humaneness is" (7.1)

While Kongzi heavily based his understanding and use of humaneness on words and ideas already in existence at his time, we yet must not undervalue his contribution to the concept. Kongzi developed the first systematic approach to humaneness and emphasized its social importance. Before Kongzi, humaneness remained on a level parallel with other aspects of morality, all generally viewed with equal importance. In the *Lunyu*, it first became the dominant ethical concept, serving both as an avenue for self-cultivation and as an indicator of moral maturity. Cai Yuanpei argues that for Kongzi humaneness "governs all other virtues" (1970). This is the new status Kongzi bestows on humaneness.

Generally speaking, Kongzi's concept of humaneness expresses three important qualities that, along with other implications, elevate it to its predominant position. The first is its heavy emphasis on ties of kinship as expressed in the connection of filial piety and humaneness. Second is its highly humanistic spirit. The third, and perhaps most importantly, is the extent to which humaneness connotes or even becomes equivalent to moral cultivation. These three elements speak broadly to almost every aspect of Confucian morality, making humaneness its central idea. This ambitious breath of scope, however, seems to give Kongzi difficulty clearly defining the concept.

Kongzi's discussion of humaneness includes many especially difficult passages, some of which appear to conflict with one another. Sometimes it seems that humaneness arises from the individual and can be attained easily. Kongzi says, "I want to be humane, and there it is" (7.30), and, "To be humaneness comes from oneself" (12.1). Most of the time, however, humaneness is said to require much more, existing on a level of morality that people may find difficult to achieve. Indeed, when Sima Niu 司马牛 asks Kongzi about humaneness, the master replies succinctly and definitively, "it is difficult" (12.3).

As a type of cultivation of individual character, humaneness also includes many different aspects of moral sentiment. While these elements are not necessarily incompatible, it can be difficult to understand their connection. The *Lunyu* records Kongzi's comment, "The unyielding, resolute, simple, and modest are close to humaneness" (13.27). However Kongzi also says, "Being able to follow five qualities anywhere [and at any time], this is humaneness. . . . [They are] deference, tolerance, sincerity, intelligence, and kindness" (17.6). In addition to these characteristics, humaneness embodies a humanistic love for others, and yet at the same time demands adherence to a patriarchal clan system. It is, thereby, an extremely complex concept that includes numerous conflicting and even contradictory elements.

Modern Readings

Feng Youlan comments on how Kongzi unites seemingly conflicting ideas. "The 'love' that Kongzi talks about is a type of feudal ideology. It is intertwined with feudal class structure and the patriarchal system. . . . One of the most important functions of Kongzi's humaneness is advocating a type of patriarchal morality, solidifying male control in the family"(1986: 107-08). This brings up another point where Kongzi's description of humaneness is inconsistent. Kongzi espouses that humaneness involves "loving everyone" (12.22). Yet the *Lunyu* also asks, "Are filial piety and fraternal reverence not the root of humaneness?" (1.2).

This uses blood relations to reduce "loving everyone" to a qualified version of universal love categorized by degrees (Feng 1986: 114). Kongzi's idea of love based on degrees and its support of the feudal clan system is what makes Kongzi's humaneness standout against Laozi's "kindness" or "affection" (*ci*) and Mozi's "indiscriminate love" (*jian'ai* 兼爱). Neither Laozi nor Mozi accept notions of degree or class difference as relevant to morality. Tong Shuye emphasizes that "the disparity between Moist and Confucian [conceptions of love] is a difference of advancement and backwardness, new and old" (1982: 16).

The restrictions placed on Kongzi's humaneness by patriarchal and feudal ideology become especially pronounced in its conflicting relationship with the rites. As Hou Wailu comments,

> Kongzi's idea of humaneness is similar to his idea of the rites. This creates a contradiction in his thought. Generally, humaneness is a moral concept that is attributed to the people, but in specific circumstances, focusing on social institutions, Kongzi attributes humaneness only to the exemplary person [i.e., ruler or nobleman].
>
> In the former case, Kongzi uses abstract ideas to restore humaneness to its psychological factors. For the latter, Kongzi uses historical conditions to tack humaneness onto the traditional [patriarchal-feudal] system. (Hou, Zhao, and Du 1957: 156)

Kongzi explains humaneness as a feeling that begins in one's heart-and-mind, whereas the rites serve as a standard system of behavior. The rites place external restrictions on people, whereas humaneness is primarily internal. Even as Kongzi praises it as the most important aspect of morality, though, he bounds it within the framework of rites. In saying, "to restrict oneself and return to the rites [or propriety], that is humaneness," (12.1), Kongzi places humaneness subordinate to the rites (Pang 1984: 32; Hu 1983: 238). This impairs the aspects of universal quality of humaneness as "loving others." Kongzi's followers do not believe that everyone's love is equal, but rather that people should be allotted different types and amounts of love based on their social position (Pang 1984: 19)

Contemporary scholars have characterized Kongzi's humaneness, using a variety of newer ideas that have largely ignored the role of the rites. Some have related humaneness to sincere feelings, psychological factors, self-awareness, and rational praxis.[10] These can be valued as unique viewpoints of various academicians or as developments in the study of humaneness. They also unavoidably influence our understandings of the ancient texts. Taking myself, for example, when reading Kongzi's, "The wise take pleasure in water; the virtuous take pleasure in mountains" (6.23), I understand the first part as embodying a romantic spirit and the latter as rational principles, much like Nietzsche's Apollo and Dionysus.

Despite its limitations through the rites and its submission to family and class relations, Kongzi's humaneness has exerted a significant impact on Chinese history and culture. In addition, it offers the world a unique and thought-provoking model of moral theory. Its contribution should not be overlooked or underemphasized in either history or today: it remains influential and presents alternatives to Western ethical thought.

Conclusion

In terms of epistemology, Laozi's "calm observation," "thorough examination," and dialectical methodology have exerted a deep impact on Chinese thought. As a pioneer of dialectical thinking in China, he also developed Chinese philosophy's broadest and deepest theory of universal patterns of change. As a government official, Laozi saw the social vicissitudes of the Spring and Autumn period firsthand, and his dialectical understanding directly responded to these experiences. Four major themes characterize this aspect of his thought:

1. Contrary objects and concepts rely on one another and their relationship of opposition to exist.
2. Opposites will change into one another.
3. When something develops to its extreme, it takes on the characteristics of its opposite.
4. There is a strong focus on the preconditions or signs for development toward an opposite state.

---

[10] Sincere feelings (*zhenqing shigan* 真情实感) is Feng Youlan's explanation of humaneness (1986). He also discusses "self-awareness" (*zijue jingshen* 自觉精神), as do Xiao Shafu and Li Jinquan (2005). Psychological factors (*xinli yinsu* 心理因素) also appear in Hou Wailu's work (1998; Hou and Zhao 1957). Similarly, Li Zehou uses rational praxis (*shijian lixing* 实践理性) (1986).

Importantly, however, Laozi's dialectal thought relies on cyclical patterns, and in doing so fails to look deeply into subjective aspects of transformation or development. His thought here builds upon a similar strain in the *Yizhuan*, which finds itself limited in the same way.[11] Kongzi, in contrast, develops no such dialectical understanding at all. Hou Wailu is mistaken when he mines dialectic out of the *Lunyu* line "I knock at both ends" (9.8) by explaining, "The 'ends' are opposites or contrary, and 'knocking at both ends' is a method for knowing the contradictory nature of things" (Hou and Huang 1981: 47). Such a reading misleadingly augments the text with concepts entirely alien to its original intent, which was to express Kongzi's views on teaching and learning. The two "ends" refer in actuality to the two sides of a question or argument, and knocking at both entails fully examining both sides of an issue. No "method for knowing the contradictory nature of things" exists in Kongzi's thought—no dialectic.

In terms of knowledge, Laozi differentiates "learning" from understanding Dao. The first involves accumulating information: the more information one has, the richer their intellect becomes. Developing an appreciation of Dao, on the other hand, means trying to understand to root and entirety of all beings, which requires losing one's subjective perspective, partiality or prejudices, and desires. Laozi writes, "Devotion to learning [seeks] daily increase. Devotion to dao [seeks] daily decrease" (ch. 48). These two operate on different levels, the quest for Dao proving almost spiritual, while that for "learning" bases itself on the accumulation of worldly knowledge (Feng 1986: 57).

One learns by grasping the patterns and characteristics of the world and the various things in it—or as Laozi puts it, knowing that "words have ancestry, and affairs have sovereigns" (ch. 70). Laozi means that language should have substance, and action should have purpose. In contrast, appreciating Dao stresses introspection, experience, and self-cultivation. "Calm observation" involves all of these things, and aims to "clear away [personal distractions] and thoroughly examine [things]" (ch. 10). Understanding Dao requires a clear mind, impartiality, and calmness, otherwise one can never achieve clarity in the heart-and-mind. This does not, however, mean that Laozi is mystical or denies the importance of knowledge, emotions, and experience. On the contrary, comprehend-

---

[11] Li Xueqin writes, "The silk manuscripts of the *Yizhuan* are undoubtedly related to the state of Chu. . . . The ten sections of the *Yizhuan* are rich with dialectical thought and very similar to the *Laozi* in many aspects" (1981).

ing Dao through "thorough examination" remains rational and requires involvement in the world (Ye 1985).

Laozi puts forth "stillness" and "movement" as the major stages in Dao's activity—two concepts that went on to hugely influence Chinese philosophy. Although he emphasizes the importance of stillness, he also establishes the necessity of movement, demonstrating their complementary relationship and mutual reliance, while also seeing stillness as the foundation of movement. The influence of this type of thinking can be seen clearly in the *Yizhuan* and even more so in the thought of later Neo-Confucians, though Kongzi never touches upon this relationship.

Moreover, Laozi's naturalistic approach to politics stands in sharp opposition to Kongzi's emphasis on virtuosity and morality. For Laozi, "naturalism" means returning to the genuine and simple, protecting natural tendencies and sincere sentiments. Zhuangzi further developed this view along the idea that each being has its own inclinations and fate. The cultural influence of their thinking is immeasurable, and has gone a long way to push against the excessive dominance of moralization, which Confucians injected into Chinese society.

The roots of Confucianism's moral project can, of course, be traced back to Kongzi. He sees morality as the ultimate guideline and outcome of anything worthwhile. At one point, Kongzi summarizes the entire Shijing, saying, "The *Shijing's* three hundred or so poems can be summed up in a single saying: 'Do not consider [doing or saying] anything bad'" (2.2).

The *Shijing* contains a rich variety of poems that describe the lives of people of all classes, from longing for loved ones distanced by war to romantic love. To say that "not considering [doing or saying] anything bad" captures the meaning of all of these poems absurdly oversimplifies one of the world's most classic collections of verse. Kongzi does so in order to establish a morality that overpowers all and encapsulates the entirety of life. This monomaniacal, normative hegemony limits the perspective of the Confucian tradition and its ability to understand the realities of the world, just as it limits its understanding of the poetry in the *Shijing*.

Nevertheless, Kongzi feels that the *Shijing* is a useful tool for governance. He encourages his disciples to read poetry, as it teaches them to serve both parents and leaders (17.9). Feng Youlan accurately observes three distinct characteristics of Kongzi's treatment of the *Shijing*: conservatism, connection to morality, and the use of political function as a standard for evaluating literature (1986). Truly, each time Kongzi mentions the *Shijing,* he finds some way to tie it into politics or morality. At one point he says, "[Personal cultivation] begins with studying the *Shijing* and is established through the rites" (8.8); and, "Without studying the *Shijing,* one cannot say anything; without studying the rites, one cannot become established" (16.13).

He even directly usurps a line from the *Shijing* to serve as a metaphor for the relationship between humaneness and the rites (3.8) He makes the role of literature in general normative, saying, "broad learning through literature and limiting oneself by rites allow one to not contravene [orthodoxy-propriety]" (6.27). Wang Qixing puts it well, explaining that manacled by the rites, "the tumultuous emotions of the inner hearts of poets are unable to rush forth and elation unable to be completely divulged. It is impossible this would not impair the content of poetic expression"(1986). The excessively moralized world of the Confucians significantly inhibits literary and artistic creative impulses.

Also, Laozi and Kongzi similarly developed traditions of thought that reject and replace religion. Laozi's Dao, as the source of the universe and the natural course or tendencies of all beings, replaces the conception of an anthropomorphic creator god or gods and cedes cosmological control to the nurturing but noncontrolling ways of dao. Laozi's assertion that "the heavens and the earth are not humane" (ch. 5) indicates that the way of the cosmos is completely natural or self-so and not biased, teleological, or subject to human emotions. He thereby destroys the assumption that humans and the heavens are of the same type or kind (*tianren helei* 天人合类), and therefore anthropomorphic control of the world, putting forward in its place an atheistic point of view that challenges the then common beliefs in spirits and divination.

Kongzi, although he does see the heavens as governing worldly affairs, similarly pushes against traditional religious thinking when he advises to "respect ghosts and spirits while keeping them at a distance" (6.22), and to "not discuss the strange, powerful, disorderly, or supernatural" (7.21). While he still believes in ghosts and spirits, here and in other passages, Kongzi maintains that people need to learn first about social interaction and worldly affairs before tackling the supernatural world. When Jilu asks him about ghosts, Kongzi responds, "Without knowing how to serve humans, how can you serve ghosts?" (11.12). Jilu follows this by asking about death, and Kongzi replies, "If you do not know [how to] live, how could you know death?" This thinking, too, greatly influenced Chinese scholars and even the entirety of Chinese culture throughout the ages. Laozi and Kongzi both push against religious views of the world, each in their own way.

Finally, Laozi and Kongzi differed greatly in their personalities and outlooks. While Kongzi proves extremely lofty-minded and uses himself as an exemplar of great virtuosity, Laozi was first to put forth a philosophy that involved concepts of alienation as well as related feelings of social estrangement. The values he pioneered created in him a sense of social alienation that he describes quite explicitly; they arose principally because he was the first to consider problems of the alienation of phenomena in some depth. Laozi favored simplicity and became a leading exemplar of China's intellectual spirit. His assertion of the power of softness epitomizes the great tenacity of the Chinese national character; his theory of the cyclical patterns of all worldly phenomena overcame many obstacles to make profound and lasting contributions to Chinese culture. As Feng Youlan explains, this idea encouraged people to remain cautious in times of prosperity and maintain hope in those of difficulty (1997).

Chapter Three

The Early *Laozi*

In 1973, two versions of the *Laozi* were discovered outside Changsha in Hunan province: the Mawangdui versions (see Mawangdui 1974). Twenty years later, in 1993, three partial copies of the *Laozi* were excavated in Guodian, Hubei, believed to be near the site of the capital of the ancient state of Chu. The finding of the Mawangdui texts drew the attention of scholars from all over the world, and many translations were produced. The Guodian texts, however, are even more important as they date at least one hundred years before those of Mawangdui.

In the 1930s and 1940s, intellectuals such as Liang Qichao and Qian Mu 钱穆 popularized the idea that the *Laozi* was composed later than the *Lunyu*. European, American, and Japanese scholars jumped onboard as well, creating a snowball effect of mistaken dating. The recently discovered texts, however, undermine any theories that saw the *Laozi* as a post-Warring States text, and many philosophers and other academics have been quick to redate it as composed in the Spring and Autumn period.

The Guodian bamboo-strip copies show major two discrepancies with later versions. The first is in chapter 19. The transmitted text has, "Get rid of humaneness and responsibility," but the Guodian version reads, "Get rid of falsehood and deception." The second major change is in chapter 40. The standard edition reads, "Everything is born from being, and being is born from nonbeing." The Guodian text does not have the second "being," so that the passage reads, "Everything is born from being and born from nonbeing."

In 1998, the extant Guodian copies of the *Laozi*, providing the earliest record of a little less than half of the transmitted text, were compiled into a single edition and published by Wenwu in Beijing along with additional chapters called the *Taiyi shengshui* 太一生水 (The Great One Brings Forth Water). In 2003, the Shanghai Museum published another lost Daoist text, the *Hengxian* 恒先 (Constancy at First). These two works had been lost to the world for over 2,300 years. The *Taiyi shengshui* was written after the *Laozi* and contains Warring States Daoist theory on the universe and its origin. The *Hengxian* goes back to the same time, but it comments more on the development of the universe than on its origin.

Comparing these writings to Confucian works, we find that the latter are almost entirely devoted to political and moral thought. Especially in its origin, the Confucian tradition has very little if anything to say about metaphysics. The Daoists, on the other hand, often discussed metaphysical topics, especially theories of the universe. Early Chinese ontology and metaphysics are, therefore, largely attributed to Daoism, whereas Confucianism dominates ethical and political discussions. The *Taiyi shengshui* and *Hengxian* bolster these classifications.

The Guodian Versions

The *Laozi* is second only to the Bible as the most translated book in the world. Not only has it immeasurably impacted Chinese culture throughout history, its significance has, especially recently, reverberated around the globe. After the discoveries at Mawangdui and Guodian, international interest resurged. Although the Guodian version is certainly not the "original" text, it is its earliest extant copy, and has finally put to rest a decades-long debate over dating the *Laozi*, while also providing intriguing revelations regarding its content.

Five years after the recovery of the Guodian *Laozi*, in May of 1998, professors Sarah Allan and Robert G. Henricks hosted an International Conference on the Guodian *Laozi* at Dartmouth College in New Hampshire. There, I presented a paper on my first reactions to the recently excavated text. Here I expand on that essay to discuss some more developed ideas.

Early in my career, I paid little attention to either Laozi as a historical figure or to his book. My concentration focused solely on his ideas. Then, in 1984, when I returned to mainland China from Taiwan, I was astonished to find that almost every university department of Chinese philosophy or history dated the *Laozi* after Kongzi, and sometimes even later than Mengzi or Mozi. I published two essays refuting this, first "Laozi Precedes Kongzi" (1988) and soon after "A Comparison of Laozi and Kongzi's Thought" (2002). The discovery of the Guodian text added irrefutable evidence to my argument.

The most absurd dating of the *Laozi* goes back to Qian Mu, who believed that it was composed even after the *Zhuangzi*. In the West, the extremely influential A. C. Graham claimed Kongzi lived before Laozi. Both scholars relied on the work of Liang Qichao who, despite being harshly criticized for sloppy scholarship, still had a lasting impact on subsequent academics.

Historical records show that Lao Dan, who served as an official historian, was a leading scholar of his time. This is why, according to the *Lüshi chunqiu* and the *Liji*, Kongzi sought to learn from Laozi. The Daoist master was already famous in his home state of Chu, as well as other Western provinces, and his renown gradually spread to Kongzi's home in Lu. Even in areas with well-established thinkers, such as Fan Li in Yue, Laozi's ideas grew popular. In fact, it seems that almost every pre-Qin text borrows from the *Laozi,* ranging from commenting on his major ideas to actual citations. I have already outlined the details of the *Lunyu* and *Mozi*'s relationship with the *Laozi,* and we should note that other texts, including the *Guanzi, Mengzi,* and *Shenzi* 申子 (Book of Master Shen), were also influenced by Laozi. The idea that the *Laozi* could have been composed after the *Zhuangzi* is therefore ridiculous.

Upon examining the *Zhuangzi,* it becomes clear that the *Laozi* served as its important ideological foundation. In over one hundred and twenty places, the *Zhuangzi* either engages or directly refers to the content of the *Laozi.*[1] Lao Dan appears five times in the Inner Chapters, and his ideas are used in over twenty passages, most obviously where Zhuangzi uses terms like "mysterious" (*xuan* 玄) or "dark" (*ming* 冥) to describe Dao.. This shows that even the earliest parts of the *Zhuangzi* go back to after the *Laozi*. Clearly, however, this argument is no longer necessary, since the Guodian texts have proven the *Laozi* as much older than any known version of the *Zhuangzi*.

Archeologists working on the Guodian tomb judge the site to have been dug sometime toward the latter half of the Warring States period. They believe that the texts found there were copied at least a generation before that. In total, three different *Laozi* versions were recovered from the tomb, all varying in length and structure. Scholars labeled them *jia* 甲

[1] The *Zhuangzi* uses content from *Laozi* 1, 2, 4, 7, 10, 13, 15, 16, 19, 20, 21, 28, 36, 37, 38, 40, 41, 45, 48, 50, 51, 54, 55, 56, 59, 71, 79, 80, and 81. It even introduces some passages with, "Lao Dan says," "Laozi says," and "It is therefore said," even if the majority of the content is not clearly demarcated as originating in the *Laozi*.

yi 乙, and *bing* 丙, commonly A, B, and C in English. Their handwriting indicates that they were copied by three different people, and therefore that the time of their transcription may differ as well.

The extant copies of the three versions for the most part record different passages of the *Laozi*, with very little overlap in contents. Only a single section from the latter portion of what is today chapter 64 appears in both the A and C versions, C being more similar to the Mawangdui and transmitted editions. In comparison, the A version appears to have been their predecessor. This discrepancy, as well as the variation in handwriting, shows clearly that the different versions were copied from different source texts. This in turn makes it clear that there were already a number of distinct versions of the *Laozi* circulating in Chu.

As to the precise time and place the original *Laozi* was written, there are a number of possibilities. Lao Dan may have written the book while serving as an official in Zhou, present-day Luoyang 洛阳. Perhaps, as Sima Qian describes it, he penned the work as notes for a border guard when he traveled west. Laozi may even have authored it toward the end of his life while living in Chang'an 长安. Whatever the case, the fact that Laozi's text was able travel hundreds of miles to Chu where Guodian is located at a time when trade between states was difficult and dangerous shows that his ideas were broadly embraced throughout China.

The three *Laozi* copies from Guodian, when compared to the transmitted edition, differ most significantly in the chapter numbers. Scholars have debated over which numbering is correct, some believing that today's is actually the original ordering. Yu Jiaxi argues, "Ancient [Chinese] authors did not number their work. . . . They often wrote individual articles that were not strung together. The ordering of their books was something that their disciples or later scholars would do" (1985: 30-32). If we take Yu's statement to be true of the *Laozi*, then the compilation and sequencing of the chapters was probably done sometime in the latter part of the Warring States period. The Mawangdui *Laozi*, written within twenty-odd years after that, contains chapter numbers that are basically in line with today's version. We can, therefore, be fairly sure that the transmitted *Laozi* was compiled early.

Supposing the *Laozi* was written one passage at a time, without any particular sequencing by Lao Dan, clears up some of the incongruities. Differences would be due to the individuality of the transcribers, not necessarily deliberate alterations of the original work. As Yu Jiaxi explains,

> Books were often bundled together, and later scholars would copy only certain texts or parts to study. . . . Classics first spread this way. Scholars could not always comprehend the full meaning of the books they read, and would choose sections and certain texts that they felt they understood and could identify with to transcribe. This is how most ancients read and studied. Transcription was an arduous task, so people would often find a section they liked for whatever reason and copy it alone. (1985, 96-97)

We can, therefore, understand the partial completeness of the Guodian *Laozi* versions as having two causes. First, the difficulties of copying texts in those times made complete works rare; second, transcribers chose texts, or portions of texts, that suited their particular interests and intentions. Wang Bo maintains that the Guodian texts themselves give evidence to Yu's claim. He argues that the B and C versions each concentrate on their own specific topics, i.e., self-cultivation and governance. The A version, he says, can be viewed as two parts, the first like the C version revolving around political philosophy, and the second part focusing on Dao and personal cultivation.

Comparing these three copies of the *Laozi* with the later Mawangdui version and the transmitted *Daode jing*, we find that little more than the order has changed. The content remains fundamentally the same. We can thus use the Guodian discovery as proof for refuting the long-standing classification of the *Laozi* as a post-Warring States text.

Moral Values

Comparing the Guodian versions with the transmitted text, we find the content largely unchanged. Despite the innumerable editions that existed over the ages, only a few individual discrepancies appear. These changes, however, have proven of tremendous importance. Minute variations in wording belie certain central aspects of Laozi's overall philosophical mission. The most striking example of this appears between Guodian A and the transmitted text in chapter 19. Guodian A has:

> Get rid of wisdom and differentiation
> And the people will benefit a hundred fold.
> Get rid of cleverness and benefit
> A thieves and robbers will have nothing.
> Get rid of *falsity and deception*
> And the people will become filial and kind.

The transmitted version, as edited by Wang Bi 王弼 (226-249 CE) reads:

> Get rid of sages and wisdom
> And the people will benefit a hundred fold.
> Get rid of *humaneness and responsibility*
> And the people will be filial and kind.
> Get rid of cleverness and benefit
> And thieves and robbers will have nothing.

The Guodian text thus emphasizes the rejection of "falsity and deception" (*quewei qiezha* 绝伪弃诈) as a way of advocating qualities of simplicity in person and society, reflecting a well-accepted ideal in Laozi and Kongzi's time. Denouncing humaneness and responsibility, on the other hand, only became popular after the *Zhuangzi*.

This chapter, with its urging to "get rid of sages and wisdom" as well as of "humaneness and responsibility," led many scholars to believe that Laozi was criticizing Confucianism. This passage, clearly altered by later scholars, played a significant role in causing academics, especially those working in mainland China after 1949, to conclude that the *Laozi* was a rather late text.

The reality is, however, that the heated antagonism between competing schools of thought, particularly of Daoism and Confucianism, did not occur until the latter part of the Warring States period. If this chapter attacks the Confucian, and possibly Mohist, advocacy of humaneness and responsibility, as many scholars have claimed, then the original words of Laozi were altered, a theory that fits well historically. The transmitted *Laozi*'s push against sages, humaneness, and responsibility is most likely a mid-to-late Warring States addition. The original *Laozi*, on which the Guodian editions were based, lacks such a focused statement against Kongzi. The additions occurred in accord with popular post-*Zhuangzi* Daoist arguments.

Although the concepts of humaneness and kindness are commonly associated with Confucianism, the *Laozi* upholds them as well. This has been often overlooked, largely because the *Laozi*'s writing is cryptic, and often employs irony or sarcasm in making profound and complex points. Lines like "The heavens and the earth are not humane. . . . Sages are not humane" (ch. 5) have proven easy for scholars to misunderstand. Misinterpretations were especially rife following the Han dynasty, when Confucian and Daoist scholars were widely at odds with each other, and then again under the Song, when Neo-Confucians rejected both Daoism and Buddhism. All this left a lasting impact on popular understanding of Daoism, creating a general impression that the *Laozi* and *Zhuangzi* were negative and sought to abandon or at least hide from certain aspects of society—including morality.

At its roots, however, Daoism seeks to positively affect society just as much as Confucianism, inheriting the humanistic spirit and concept of "ruling by virtuosity," typical of Zhou culture. Kongzi and Mengzi were not different from Laozi and Zhuangzi in wanting to build a humanistic and moral society. This was the goal of both camps. The distinction between the two schools lies in how they believe this could be brought about, and specifically in their approaches to the establishment of human relations according to feudal ethics. While the study of their differences is, of course, tremendously important,[2] below I examine specifically the continuities between Kongzi and Laozi's thought. Understanding similarities is crucial, especially since their differences have been overstressed.

Loyalty, Sincerity, and Kindness

Like Kongzi, Laozi emphasizes loyalty and sincerity. He says, "As for the rites, shallowness of loyalty and sincerity form the beginning of disorder" (ch. 38). Laozi believes that loyalty and sincerity are essential to rites propriety, and he means to say here that the result of conducting rites insincerely is chaos in society. The lines just prior to these, from the same passage, read, "When Dao is lost, there is virtuosity. When virtuosity is lost, there is humaneness. When humaneness is lost, there is responsibility. When responsibility is lost, there are the rites" (ch. 38).

---

[2] The divergences between Laozi and Kongzi in their philosophical direction as well as the differences in the character of their thinking are very clear—a fact often ignored, consciously or unconsciously, by advocates of the idea that the two are mutually complementary. The largest distinction is that Laozi established Chinese metaphysics, including cosmology and ontology, as well as his own unique ideals of human life, making him the father of Chinese philosophy. The theories and approaches of Daoism he formed—such as methods of thinking characterized by opposition, cyclicality, the derivation of the human world from Dao, and the integrated wholeness of the heavens, the earth, and humanity—run throughout the history of Chinese philosophy. In comparison, Kongzi lacks the metaphysical and abstract in his thinking. He does, however, combine traditional ideas of the rites and humaneness to build a dominant system of ethics, making him the most influential figure in Chinese morality and politics.

These lines have misled many scholars into thinking that Laozi believes Dao and virtuosity are more important than humaneness, responsibility, and rites, whereas in truth virtuosity, humaneness, responsibility, and rites are all included in Dao. When differentiated, they can be understood in the cited sequence, meaning that losing touch with their source (i.e., Dao) creates a chain reaction of decline. People aligning themselves with Dao means they have virtuosity, which manifests in human relations as humaneness, responsibility, and the rites.

Putting this passage in context, therefore, shows that Laozi does not reject humaneness, responsibility, or even the rites. What he opposes is the highly formalized rites that have separated from Dao and lost their inherent meaning. Hanfeizi, the earliest known commentator on the *Laozi* and most famous proponent of the Legalist school, explains, "Rites are the performance of emotions. Culture is the display of character" (20.6). In other words, the rites have two sides: their internal substance of emotions and character, plus their outward performance and display. Laozi emphasized their substance and accordingly believes that their practice requires deep sincerity.

Laozi's moral grounding begins with three so-called treasures—kindness, frugality, and lack of strife. These are clearly all directed at greedy rulers and officials, forming a way to criticize them for starting wars and causing social disorder merely to serve their avarice.

Kindness actually includes connotations of humaneness. Laozi writes, "The heart-and-mind is excellent if it is still. Relations are excellent if they are humane. Words are excellent if they are reliable. Government is excellent if it creates order. Affairs are excellent if they get things done. Actions are excellent if they are done at the appropriate time" (ch. 8). This presents a process that moves from self-cultivation outward toward proper engagement in political affairs, making humaneness and sincerity important pre-requisites for successful human interaction. In this aspect, Laozi and Kongzi have very similar perspectives on how to be a good member of society.

Along with treasuring kindness, Laozi also advocates filial piety. The *Laozi* mentions this in the eighteenth chapter, where filial piety is coupled with humaneness and responsibility. The Guodian version reads:

> When the great Dao is abandoned,
> There come from it humaneness and responsibility.
> When the six relations are not in harmony
> There comes from them filial love.

When the country is in disorder,
There come from it upright ministers.

The transmitted text, on the other hand, reads:

When the great Dao is abandoned,
There come humaneness and responsibility.
When the wise and intelligent appear,
There comes hypocrisy.
When the six relations are not in harmony,
There comes filial piety.
When the country is in disorder,
There come loyal ministers" (ch. 18).

The addition of the second line in the later version has led scholars to see humaneness and responsibility as parallel to hypocrisy (with filial love and ministers as a separate pair), and therefore as viewed negatively by Laozi. The absence of this line in the Guodian text shows humaneness and responsibility as originally one of three parallel positive outcomes, which further accords with the three parallel lines of the following chapter—chapters 17-19 traditionally forming a single unit.

Originally, then, humaneness and responsibility were included as aspects of Dao, naturally and harmoniously integrated with Dao just as filial piety is part of the harmony of the six relations. With its breakdown, filial piety becomes a valuable, positive force. In the same way, with the loosening of social norms, conduct of true humaneness and responsibility becomes rare and highly prized.

The Guodian text shoes no rejection of humaneness and responsibility or devaluation of filial love. The later manipulation of this chapter with the addition of the second line was probably due to Zhuangzi's influence, as the *Zhuangzi* is much more negative when it comes to humaneness and responsibility.

Zhuangzi's Impact

Zhuangzi criticizes humaneness and responsibility principally for their use as tools of the upper classes and for formalizing human relations, stripping them of meaningful expression. Zhuangzi is not, however, critical of humaneness and responsibility in themselves. If properly understood and practiced, he is actually in favor of them.

The *Zhuangzi* records, "Great Dao cannot be spoken of. . . . Great humaneness does not [consider itself] humane. . . . Humaneness when constant is not all encompassing" (2.10). Here we see that Zhuangzi believes that true humaneness is impartial. He distances his understanding from the Confucians, which the *Mengzi* epitomizes in the line, "Loving relatives, that is humaneness" (6B23). The Confucian depiction of humaneness is largely defined by blood relations, and Zhuangzi's statement that "common humaneness is not all-encompassing" aims to criticize just such confinement of humaneness to a limited group or clan. Humaneness should also be humble. That "great humaneness" does not see or display itself as virtuous or moral means that truly humane conduct does not cause pride or boasts.

The passage presents great Dao first, then great humaneness, which shows the latter residing in Dao and forming one aspect of it. The *Zhuangzi* says that a great master "blends all beings harmoniously, but does not claim to be responsible from them; he benefits everything in the world, but does not claim to be humane" (6.8). The idea of blending or benefiting everything is a reflection of Laozi's proposal that "virtuosity nourishes all beings" (ch. 51). Zhuangzi agrees with Laozi's advocacy of not acting assertively, which posits that Dao carries humaneness and responsibility out naturally but not overtly in the manifest world.

Zhuangzi's Dao, like Laozi's, is a metaphysical concept. In the actual world, it manifests as humane and responsible conduct, but this happens without explicit intention or effort. One of the most famous passages in the *Zhuangzi* is about "sitting and forgetting" (6.9). It describes Yan Hui in conversation with Kongzi. Yan learns to "forget" Confucian values at the encouragement of his teacher Kongzi, including humaneness and responsibility as well as rites and music. Through this "forgetting," Yan arrives at a state of ultimate accordance with his environment. His "forgetting" does not disregard humaneness and responsibility; rather, it makes him so comfortable in their practice that he no longer has to think about them.

The *Zhuangzi* further describes reaching this level of automatic humane and responsible conduct in a story about Dang questioning Zhuangzi about the highest level of humaneness. Zhuangzi replies, "The highest level of humaneness is impartial." Dang then asks about the relationship between humaneness and filial piety, and Zhuangzi responds:

> Filial respect is easy; filial love is difficult. Filial love is easy; forgetting about relatives is difficult. Forgetting about relatives is easy; making relatives forget about oneself is difficult. Making relatives forget about oneself is easy; also forgetting the world is difficult. Also forgetting the world is easy; also making the world forget oneself is difficult. (14.2)

Zhuangzi here provides an explicit hierarchy of "easiest" to most "difficult." At the lowest level is being filial through respect, topped successively by being filial through love, giving one's parents a comfortable and stable life, making sure they do not worry, setting the world at ease, and ultimately having the world forget about oneself. Clearly Zhuangzi advocates humaneness, responsibility, kindness, and filial piety to the point of "forgetting"—a state in which they occur without effort. This is the unique approach, through which he values these qualities.

These discussions enhance the understanding of the positive aspects of Zhuangzi's view of humaneness and responsibility. His criticisms of these concepts usually occur in opposition to rulers, who use morality to shackle people's hearts-and-minds intellectually. Zhuangzi's followers, some of whom added to the text, criticized the use of morality as a political tool—a message that became increasingly prevalent in the late Warring States period in reaction to the growing rigidity of the social order.

The Outer Chapters of the *Zhuangzi*, attributed to his later disciples, show two distinct views of humaneness and responsibility. One carries forward the idea that the highest form of humaneness is when it mysteriously combines with Dao. The *Tiandi* chapter records, "Loving people and benefiting things is called humaneness. . . . [Sages of old] were upright and did the correct thing, without knowing that it was responsibility. They loved one another without knowing that it was humaneness" (12.2, 13).

The other view criticizes crooked officials and social institutions that bolster themselves with these concepts. Its representatives condemn moral teaching, because "calling for humaneness and responsibility causes disruption and chaos in the world" (8.2). To them, intentional morality is problematic. They also harshly oppose rulers who "use humaneness and responsibility to tangle people's hearts-and-minds" (11.2). The most poignant and perhaps most famous comment of this view is:

> [If we teach people] to be proud of being humaneness and responsibility, then [we teach them] to steal based on them. How can I know this? One who steals a buckle for his belt is put to death, yet one who steals a country

is made a prince. At the princes gate is where humaneness and responsibility exist. (10.2)

In fact, this saying became quite popular among common people in ancient China, proving the strong influence the *Zhuangzi* had on late Warring States peasants. This passage is not only directed at Confucian scholars, but also at Mohist thinkers. Against this background, then, an anonymous intellectual or transcriber altered the *Laozi* to advocate "getting rid of humaneness and responsibility."

We now see clearly that certain lines in the transmitted *Laozi* were changed to fit late Warring States ideologies. In fact, these changes were most likely a direct result of the influence of the Outer Chapters of the *Zhuangzi*. Millennia later, the altered lines became central to some scholars' arguments that the entirety of the *Laozi* was composed in this later era. The discovery of the Guodian texts, however, shows that opposition to humaneness and responsibility did not exist in earlier versions of the *Laozi*, and therefore that these arguments, weak as they already were, can be dismissed completely.

Philosophical Development

Of the three *Laozi* versions discovered at Guodian, version A seems to be the closest to the original and presents scholars with the greatest challenges. There are four major discrepancies between Guodian A and the transmitted text.

1. Guodian A begins with what is today *Laozi* 19 and shows that several lines opposing Confucian morality, including humaneness and responsibility, were mistakenly attributed to Laozi, who originally made statements against falsity, deception, and differentiation. The altered lines of the transmitted text are quite negative and led *Laozi* followers to reject a huge part, if not all, of the ethical concepts of humaneness and responsibility, which were once native to Laozi's philosophy. Guodian A, at this time allows us to reestablish the *Laozi*'s view on morality.

2. It contains lines similar to *Laozi* 16, but they include the notion of "guarding the middle." This is worth particular scholarly attention, since as it was later replaced and went unexplored for thousands of years as an aspect of Daoist thought.

3. Guodian A, matching *Laozi* 57, records, "The more tools of justice are displayed, the more robbers and thieves there will be." In today's

edition, the word "legislation" (*faling* 法令) replaces "tools of justice" (*fawu* 法物). Consequently, there is a tradition of scholarship that argues Laozi rejects legal measures. The original wording of "tools of justice," though, does not necessarily denote law per se, which means that this idea also needs to be analyzed anew.

4. Through Guodian A matching *Laozi* 40, we now know that Laozi originally saw being and nonbeing as equal images of Dao. The subsequent ordering of this relationship in the statement, "Everything in the world was born from being, and being was born from nonbeing" was formative during the Dark Learning (*xuanxue* 玄学) movement of the Wei-Jin period, when Wang Bi proposed that nonbeing was more ontologically fundamental than being. This started a long philosophical debate about the relationship between the two. Guodian A provides a better look at Laozi's original meaning and reframes Wang Bi's assertion and the controversy surrounding it.

The Middle Way

Both Daoism and Confucianism assert the importance of "the middle" (*zhong* 中). While scholars have often focused on this aspect of Confucian texts, they tend to ignore similar passages in Daoism. Fortunately, however, the Guodian *Laozi* explicitly advocates "guarding the middle" (*shou zhong* 守中), compelling academics to reevaluate the significance of "the middle way" in Daoism.

In addition to the citation in Guodian A matching *Laozi* 16 noted above, the text also contains a phrase about guarding the middle, equally found in the transmitted text. It says, "Abundance of words [commands] lead to exhaustion; they are inferior to guarding the middle" (ch. 5). The repetition of "guarding the middle" in the Guodian version, however, shows that this was a concept of particular significance for Laozi.

While the middle way in Confucianism consists of being impartial and avoiding extremes in all aspects of one's conduct, for Daoists, it generally means a having pure and simple mentality. Guodian A places "guarding the middle" alongside "concentrating on emptiness" (ch. 16). Both "middle" and "empty" refer to a mental state. Later Huang-Lao Daoists of the Jixia Academy's inherited this idea, as seen in the *Guanzi*'s repeated mentioning of the "middle." It notes, "Rest one's heart-mind on the middle" (49.3); and "The correct heart-mind rests in the middle" (49.4). Here the "middle" describes a condition in which the heart-and-mind is free of worry, properly oriented, still and quiet. The *Guanzi* stresses harmony in the human heart-and-mind again when says, "Returning peacefully to the middle, physical expression and temperament nurture each other" (38.10).

Confucians and Daoists both are hugely concerned with harmony. Early Confucians talked a great deal about harmony in social relations in particular, whereas Daoists focused more on harmony within an individual's heart-and-mind. The *Zhuangzi* mentions both, linking social harmony and harmony in the heart-and-mind with cosmic harmony and systematically discoursing on the continuity between these three (Chen 2011).

According to the *Laozi*, the middle is something that must be protected or guarded. Zhuangzi similarly comments on the middle, but he says it should be cultivated (*yangzhong* 养中). Like Laozi, he also uses "middle" to refer to mental harmony. Except a single instance of epistemological usage in the second chapter, where the middle describes the "pivot of Dao" (*daoshu* 道枢), every mention of "middle" here relates to the heart-and-mind. An emphasis on cultivating a pureness of the heart-and-mind appears in the lines, "[The heart-and-mind] is in harmony [*zhong*], pure and honest, when it has returned to feelings [natural qualities] (*qing* 情)" (15.1).

Later, the term "respecting the middle" (*jingzhong* 敬中) refers to the heart-and-mind's empty "middle," i.e., balance: "When one stays free of anxiety to maintain the vitality of their heart-and-mind, and respects the middle to interact with others . . . one's spirit altar will be maintained" (24.8). Zhuangzi here refers to the highest degree of personal cultivation as a "spirit altar" (*lingtai* 灵台), which he in other places calls "spirit mansion" (*lingfu* 灵府) (5.4). When the heart-and-mind's spirit has been cultivated enough to reach the level of "spirit alter" or "spirit mansion," it plays a passive role in defending one's heart-and-mind against changes in the world.

People at this level no longer allow external turmoil to upset them or disrupt their internal balance, which also has the positive effect of allowing one to maintain a cheerful state of mind when approaching the external world and of feeling in harmony with all beings. This type of appreciation for one's environment was later embraced in the realm of aesthetics as a harmonious blend of spirit/consciousness and physical form. The cultivation of the middle allows for one to achieve a state in which one's "heart-and-mind rides on the things of the word, wandering [carefree]" (4.3)

From Laozi to Huang-Lao

The "middle" for Laozi and Zhuangzi is a state of balance in the heart-and-mind. Later Huang-Lao Daoists took this and externalized it, shifting from the internal harmony of "middle" to an emphasis on physical balance of "degree" (*du* 度).

In the *Guanzi*, the notion of the middle is entirely analogous to that in the *Laozi* and *Zhuangzi*, emphasizing inner harmony. The *Huangdi sijing*, a product of scholarship closely related to that of the *Guanzi* and written around the same time, generally focuses more on how to have sagely interactions with others.[3] Therefore, despite both being regarded as representatives of Huang-Lao Daoism, the two works are very different. The *Guanzi* speaks of the middle in terms of the heart-and-mind, while the *Huangdi sijing* looks at external "degree." The latter's shift toward the external is among its most important characteristics and essential to the development of Dao-based concepts of legality. "Degree" here refers to the degree to which Dao-based law is carried out. The "Daoyuan" 道源 chapter of the *Huangdi sijing* says, "Keep in line with Dao and proceed [implementing law] by degrees." This closely relates to the "balancing of power" (*quanheng* 权衡) found in its *Jingfa* 经法 part.

The Huang-Lao conception of law and moral code as arising out of Dao represents a significant development within Daoist thought. This breakthrough was driven by the demands of the times, yet also retains theoretical aspects that can be traced to earlier sources. Laozi's own Dao already harbors an essence of practical objectivity, which easily provides the foundation for social codes among later thinkers, including those of Huang-Lao Daoism. Laozi also imbues Dao with a common generality that the Huang-Lao thinkers use for their moral theories, as well—again showing a developmental thread running between the two.

---

[3] Analyzing this more deeply, we see the "Neiye" and "Xinshu shang" chapters of the *Guanzi* as working in two different directions. The first focuses on mastery of inner sagacity and cultivation of the body, while the latter looks instead toward governance. This focus on governance is similar to that of the *Huangdi sijing*, which makes me believe it is possible both works are products of the state of Qi's Jixia Academy, although most scholars believe the latter work to originate from the state of Chu.

Translator's note: Here the author is comparing the *Guanzi* as guidance for achieving the state of an "inner sage" (*neisheng* 内圣) with the *Huangdi sijing* as a text for "outer kings" (*waiwang* 外王).

Laozi's rejection of particularly harsh legal punishments probably resulted from witnessing the corruption of a society built upon strong governance, but this does not mean that he necessarily rejected less extreme uses of law. The transmitted *Laozi* has, "The more laws and decrees are displayed, the more robbers thieves there will be" (ch. 57). Many scholars have used this citation to argue that Laozi was not in favor of establishing laws or regulations. The Guodian and Mawangdui versions of the *Laozi*, however, differ from the later transmitted text in wording, recording "tools of justice" in place of "laws and decrees" An annotation attributed to the founding master of Huang-Lao Daoism, Heshang Gong 河上公, notes that the term that appears to mean "tools of justice" actually refers to "precious things."[4] If this is true, then Laozi's original meaning was not in opposition to legislation, but rather provided the base for Huang-Lao Daoism, which saw laws as assisting in carrying out Dao in the human sphere.

Being and Nonbeing

In Laozi's thought, being (*you*) and nonbeing (*wu*) form a pair of ontological categories, both referring to Dao. *Laozi* 1 speaks of being and nonbeing as aspects of Dao, said to "arise together yet being of different names." They describe Dao as simultaneously metaphysical and of the manifest world. *Laozi* 2 and 11 go on to discuss the being and nonbeing of things in the phenomenal world, filling out an epistemological theory that sees opposites as complementary and forming a complete whole.

The transmitted *Laozi* further contains an altered version of chapter 40, saying, "being is born from nonbeing." This has led to great difficulties in understanding the text, as it seems to posit nonbeing as more primordial than being—in sharp contradiction to the opening chapter's identification of them arising together:

> Transmitted version: "Everything is born from being, and being is born from nonbeing."
> Guodian version: "Everything is born from being and born from nonbeing."

The difference is just the single character *you*, but the philosophical implications are huge. The transmitted *Laozi* discusses the origin of all

---

[4] Jiang Xichang and Gao Ming both maintain this. See Gao 1996: 106.

phenomena, whereas the Guodian text makes an ontological statement. Looking at the rest of the *Laozi*, the latter proves a much better fit. Most conspicuous is the transmitted version's contradiction, "The nameless (*wuming* 无名) is the beginning of the heavens and the earth. The named (*youming* 有名) is the mother of all beings" (ch. 1). Here both the nameless and named equally refer to Dao; they are different aspects of the same entity. This statement is in line with the Guodian version of chapter 40, but it conflicts significantly with that of the transmitted text. This alteration led to much difficulty and confusion in interpreting the *Laozi*.

Laozi's metaphysical discussion of being and nonbeing continued in the Wei-Jin period, a fundamental topic in Dark Learning. Wang Bi and others developed this sequential relationship between the two into one between a more primordial and alter state, a division into noumena and phenomena. Here nonbeing is the metaphysical underpinning of all beings in existence—or being—and exists on the truest ontological level, from which being is omitted. In other words, only nonbeing is Dao. This theory, explicated in Wang Bi's commentary on the *Laozi*, became the standard for interpretations of Daoism.

Dark Learning championing nonbeing in due course produced reactionary arguments that supported the primacy of being, as for example by Pei Wei 裴頠 (263-300). Later, the Eastern Jin scholar and Buddhist monk Sengzhao 僧肇 (374-414) proved even more radical, believing that neither being nor nonbeing existed. In the much later Neo-Confucian movement of the Song and Ming, thinkers discussed "the extreme of nonbeing becoming the extreme of being" in continuation of the argument for the birth of being from nonbeing.

The discovery of the Guodian *Laozi* now shows that being and nonbeing were originally parallel or equal in their relationship, forming two basic aspects of Dao. The question, which of them is more primordial, is therefore moot. The subsequent addition of a second "being" in the transmitted text made the relationship between being and nonbeing problematic and disrupted the original unity of Laozi's system of thought. Wang Bi's insistence on nonbeing as more original, creating a "root and branches" relationship between the two, has led scholars to argue that being is just another word for phenomena and that nonbeing refers to Dao, subordinating being to nonbeing. This stands in direct contradiction to the *Laozi*'s opening chapter—a conflict that the Guodian *Laozi* shows did not exist in the original version. Now that the Guodian texts are available, the original importance of being should be taken into account in all further research.

Feng Youlan recognized the conflict between chapters 1 and 40 prior to the Guodian discovery. He dealt with it by claiming that the statement, "being is born from nonbeing," refers to logical rather than chronological order (1997). My own explanation in reconciling the chapters has long been that nonbeing and being both refer to Dao; they discuss the way Dao proceeds from formlessness to form. The Guodian discovery supports such a reading and finally clears up centuries of confusion.

Issues in the Guodian *Laozi*

Besides the three partial versions of the *Laozi*, the Guodian find also included several other texts, including a previously lost work called the *Taiyi shengshui* as well as the *Zhongxin zhi dao* 忠信之道 (The Way of the Loyal and Faithful), a mixture of Daoist and Confucian ideas with a strong inclination toward Laozi's thought. The works are extremely short, but their philosophical implications could not be greater, providing serious grounds for rewriting Chinese intellectual history.

With the discovery of the Guodian texts, all arguments for a later dating of the composition of the *Laozi* were immediately overturned by hard scientific evidence. This cemented Laozi's place in Chinese history as an original and pioneering thinker. In terms of philosophical content, there are two major points where the Guodian *Laozi* differs from the transmitted text. In addition to resolving the ontological relationship between being and nonbeing as shown above, the lack of the line telling us to "get rid of humaneness and responsibility" reflects Laozi's original nondismissive attitude toward these concepts. Further aspects of these issues need to be considered, with paramount importance for the history of Chinese philosophy.

From the Spring and Autumn period to the end of the Warring States, China saw the creation of many different schools of thought. Laozi became a pioneer of Chinese philosophy by proposing new philosophical theories, kicking off a period ripe with philosophical breakthroughs. His position as a founder of Chinese philosophy was confirmed first by his influence during his own lifetime, when Laozi was Kongzi's teacher and perhaps even friend, as is well documented. Laozi clearly influenced the *Lunyu*. Approaching their relationship philosophically, we see that when Kongzi says, "I transmit, but do not invent," he does not claim that he has made no intellectual contribution, but refers to the fact that he wishes to carry on the Zhou traditions. Laozi, on the other hand, breaks from the Zhou and incorporates cosmology and personal cultivation into a comprehensive and unified metaphysical system based on Dao. This is the first such deep philosophical treatment of these areas of thought in China.

Laozi's philosophical theories broke new ground in four major areas. First is in his pioneering treatment of the primordial state of the world (chs. 1, 25). Second, he broke new ground in his discussion of the creation of the universe (ch. 42). Third, although transformation was already a popular topic, Laozi was the first to look at the universe in terms of processes of change (chs. 20, 40). Finally, he was first to posit that all beings are generated from Dao (chs. 14, 21).

Not surprisingly, then, when we look at Chinese philosophy in terms of its general themes and concepts—be it the universe, ontology, Dao, or change—we find its main focal points were introduced by Laozi and its development has followed the paths he set (Zhang 1958). This is especially clear in Han texts on the origin of the universe and morality. It is further apparent in the Wei-Jin period, when scholars focused largely on ontology. A few hundred years after that, Laozi's work proved highly influential again when Neo-Confucians under the Song and Ming integrated the comprehensive metaphysical system of Laozi's cosmology and ontology. His philosophical system provided a foundational breakthrough in its time, which has influenced the entire course of Chinese philosophy.

Surveying the recent scholarship on China's intellectual history, Hu Shi appears as the only prominent scholar, who does not make the mistake of believing Kongzi was the first philosopher. His major publication on the topic, however, failed to have much impact in academia, mainly because it does not actually discuss philosophical problems (1989). Feng Youlan, who is much more philosophical, became extremely influential, but unfortunately his historical understanding was biased toward cultural issues rather than philosophical ones, causing him to make mistakes in the chronology of the scholarly thought. By the time he released his *Zhongguo zhexueshi xinbian*, Feng had begun to concentrate on philosophical issues more in his account of history; however, he maintained a historical view based on a linear and scientific model (1986: 105).[5] His historical assertions remained incorrect, but they were widely accepted.

---

[5] In the original version of his work, Feng repeatedly refers to Kongzi as carrying on the work of the King Wen of Zhou and his son, the Duke of Zhou,

Feng's mistaken dating of the pre-Qin thinkers influenced the great works on the history of philosophy of the 20th century, misleading almost every scholar in mainland China, Hong Kong, and Taiwan into believing that Kongzi lived before Laozi. Considering the discovery of the Guodian *Laozi,* which serves as scientific evidence against this claim, as well as the decisive influence of Laozi's philosophy on the course of Chinese intellectual history, it is essential that we rectify the mistaken assumption that Kongzi preceded Laozi.

Morality

The Guodian selections of the *Laozi* portray an approach to humaneness and responsibility that is quite different from what we find in the transmitted text. As mentioned above, Laozi's view of these ethical concepts needs to be reevaluated based on the earlier version of chapter 19. Comparing the two, it is obvious that the Guodian's line fits better with the concepts in popular circulation during Laozi and Kongzi's time.

This allows us to reflect on further points of Chinese intellectual history. In addition to helping overturn the long-standing theory that Kongzi was born before Laozi, the later alteration of chapter 19 also shows that Laozi, like Kongzi, had a moral philosophy. The difference between the two lies in the details of their theories. Laozi, too, maintains the importance of humaneness and responsibility, but his understanding of them is much broader than Kongzi's.

In his philosophical system, Laozi uses several styles of argument to discuss morality. For one, he employs a type of inverse presentation of his thought in which positive appears negative (*zhengyan ruofan* 正言若反). For another, he understands human life almost always from a cosmological perspective. Then again, he talks about the way of the world, or the heavens, and the way of humanity as following the same general principles. Laozi lays out his view on humaneness and responsibility through the interplay of these three approaches. In chapter 8, he says clearly that humaneness is key to successful human interaction. When he discusses humaneness on the larger level of the heavens and the earth, however, he approaches them through the more complex lens of inverse argumentation. He takes a view that extends beyond humanity to elevate

---

looking at Kongzi's historical position from a cultural rather than a philosophical persepective.

humaneness as a quality characteristic to a generative universal power, reaching beyond the heart-and-mind and human intentionality.

Laozi often views humanity from the heavenly realm (*tiandi jingjie* 天地境界), a phrase from Feng Youlan's theory of the "four realms of life" (2007). This realm is the highest level of human understanding and conduct, where the individual works consciously for the betterment and benefit of all beings. Here people use the limitlessness of Dao to dissolve the limitations arising from restraints of the human heart-and-mind. Laozi then applies humaneness and responsibility on this cosmic level.

Fundamentally, Laozi inherits the humanistic concerns of the Western Zhou, including the ethics of humaneness, responsibility, and sincerity that formed the core of its culture of rites. Building on these concepts, his cosmological perspective and idealistic quest to loosen the restraints of the heart-and-mind made him elevate humaneness to a cosmological level. When he says, "The heavens and the earth are not humane; they take all beings as straw dogs" (ch. 5), he denies a cosmological humaneness, but in fact implies recourse to beneficence and virtuosity that contain humaneness on a level that surpasses the human heart-and-mind. This is the level of the cosmos in its disinterested generative capacity. From this perspective, the supposed denial of the humaneness of the cosmos undergoes Laozi's inverse argumentation of the positive appearing negative; it thereby affirms humaneness in the vital unfolding of phenomena in the world.

Zhuangzi understood this level of Laozi's concept of humaneness, and provided an even clearer interpretation as not something that involves kindness, virtuosity, or wisdom, but rather as something expressed through the disinterested generative capacity of Dao, "whose beneficence is immeasurable but does not enact humaneness" (6.8). Dao's beneficence expresses itself formlessly, in a way that humans cannot adequately comprehend, through the natural or self-so development of all beings in the manifest world. They each follow their own paths, while growing and transforming of themselves.

This is the general picture of agreement and divergence in the understanding of humaneness between Daoists and Confucians. The differences occur on three different levels.

Divergences

1. Cosmos. Laozi sees the sage as in complete accord with, and even modeled on, cosmological Dao. This is why the sage is just like the heavens and the earth in being "not humane." He models the sage's heart-and-mind on Dao: the sage should rely neither on personal preferences nor on external, emotional triggers in making decisions. His sage "does not have an invariable heart-and-mind; he takes the people's hearts-and-minds as his own" (ch. 49)

The claim that the heavens and the earth are "not humane" relates directly to the idea that "Dao consistently engages in non-assertive action" (ch. 37). Denying the attribution of humaneness to the heavens and the earth confirms that the cosmos does not consciously strive to attain this (or any) ideal. Yet, although devoid of human intention and any moral imperative, the cosmos possesses a limitless life-giving, generative capacity. This creative power unfolds on the very foundation of the cosmos's universal absence of its own intentionality. The efficacy of the sage embodies this "great humaneness" of cosmic creation and transformation.

2. Humanity. Laozi says, "The heavens and the earth are not humane," yet he also asserts that people should be humane in their interactions with others. While the cosmos lacks human intentionality and a particular heart-and-mind, people possess hearts-and-minds that are capable of humaneness and should therefore engage it in the human sphere.

Laozi's denial of humaneness to the cosmos but advocacy of humaneness in human interaction is, therefore, not as contradictory as it may first appear. Sages model themselves on the cosmos, approaching the world humbly and through non-assertive action in order to avoid the interference of subjectivity or acts of coercion. Laozi also recognizes the social necessity of humaneness and kindness among the people.

Zhuangzi follows these ideas, taking the cosmological view that "great humaneness is not humaneness" (2.10) and that "utmost humaneness is impartial" (14.2). However, he reflects in more extended detail on the importance of humaneness and responsibility. In the "Gengsang Chu" chapter (ch. 23), he contemplates family relations. He notes: stepping on a stranger's foot in the marketplace necessitates an apology; stepping on the foot of a younger sibling calls for tender care; stepping on the foot of one's own child requires no contrition at all. Seen in the light of the *Laozi,* shows the ethical context where "utmost humaneness is impartial."[6] This is also the view expressed in the passage, "[Sages of old] were upright and correct without knowing that it was responsibility. They loved one another without knowing that it was humaneness" (*Zhuangzi* 12.13). Here, the Daoist ideals of humaneness and responsibility are default, unproclaimed virtuous actions undertaken without even a shred of self-awareness.

In terms of social interaction, Zhuangzi expounds on humaneness in almost Confucian terms, saying, "Loving people and benefiting things is called humaneness" (12.2). Later, the great Song Confucian Zhu Xi uses these exact same words in his definition.

3. Constant. Laozi and Zhuangzi often use negative presentation to express positive meaning, penetrating into the subtle aspects of things in order to touch upon meaning at deep, foundational levels. The addition of the line, "Get rid of humaneness and responsibility" in the transmitted *Laozi* (ch. 19) most likely was the result of Zhuangzi's influence. His own call "to reject humaneness and responsibility" (10.2), however, is not a generalized statement, but rather points directly at the shortcomings of Zhou culture.

Zhuangzi's teaching stood in open opposition to the Confucians, who advocated the continuance of Zhou political-cultural institutions as based on patriarchal clanship and blood relations. Socially, the Confucian definition of humaneness as loving one's relatives led to a system that encouraged humaneness and closeness within the family. In the political sphere, however, the close connection among clan members led to a dearth of broader political and social justice and hindered inclusive community-wide benevolence.

By the late Spring and Autumn and early Warring States periods, problems of nepotism and lazy officials were rampant all through the country. Their prevalence provoked Mozi's outcry that "relatives of princes and dukes are rich and honored without merit" (2.3.2). This was also the situation Mengzi resigned himself to when he admonished rulers to take into account the feelings of the aristocracy in their governing, noting that working in "politics is not difficult, [as long as] one does not offend important families" (4A6). This Confucian advocacy of nepotism closely connects to China's failure to develop rule of law over the follow-

---

[6] Translator's note: Presumably the implicit reasoning here runs along the lines of parents topping this hierarchy as they have created their children, and Dao transcending ethical hierarchy as the "parent" of all beings. This seems to also be what affords it impartiality as well as utmost virtuosity.

ing two millennia. It has further bred a vision of the nobility serving as parents and shepherds of the masses, deeply rooted in the minds of the upper classes over the centuries.

Zhuangzi and Mengzi's visions of humaneness illustrate the fundamental differences in their thinking. Mengzi writes, "loving relatives, that is humaneness" (6B23), whereas Zhuangzi puts forth the much more inclusive idea that "loving people and benefiting things is called humaneness" (12.2). Applying these explanations to the political realm, their implications are hugely different.

The *Zhuangzi* creates universal moral values, whereas the *Mengzi*'s definition of humaneness quickly degenerates into the glue cementing kinship to government positions. The *Zhuangzi* further adds a deeply philosophical element with the line, "Humaneness when constant is not all encompassing" (2.10), which criticizes the prejudiced and narrow Confucian restriction of humaneness to one's own clan. The discourse on Robber Zhi in the *Zhuangzi,* despite its rather extreme views, delineates the widespread and prevalent phenomenon that, when the rulers of past dynasties seized power, one saw "the methods of the wise and sagacious serving to protect robbers and thieves" (10.1)—that is, those who had snatched authority.

This reflects historical reality of the transfer of power, as those controlling political authority have proven most successful at having their speech heeded, and ethical discourse has therefore all too often denigrated into merely a tool of those in power. Zhuangzi laments:

> [If we teach people] to be proud of being humane and responsible, then [we teach them] to steal based on these virtues. How do I know this? One who steals a belt buckle is put to death, but one who steals a country is made a prince. At the prince's gate exist humaneness and responsibility. Is this not then the pilfering of humaneness, responsibility, sagacity, and wisdom? (10.2)

Zhuangzi's point resounds throughout the ages. These words of immense historical significance, moreover, were included among the Guodian bamboo manuscripts.[7]

---

[7] The *Yucong* 语从 (Thicket of Sayings) has, "One who steals a belt buckle is put to death, yet one who steals a state is made a prince, and at the prince's gate exist men of responsibility."

In pointing out the failings of institutions based on the rites, Daoists acknowledged the positive aspects of humaneness and responsibility. Kongzi and Laozi both proved pioneering in this regard. Comparing their understanding of humaneness and responsibility demonstrates the shared nature of their origin in Zhou ethics and culture, including their humanistic spirit and the idea of ruling by virtuosity. Facing the cultural crisis when rites and music collapsed in the later Spring and Autumn period, Kongzi and Laozi each sought to reestablish traditional Zhou values along the lines of their own visions.

Kongzi traced the problems back to people's moral sensibilities and laid strong foundations for rites and virtues, envisioning them as key to putting people in harmony. He used ethics as a means to affect and adjust people's consciousnesses in a positive way, to elevate their awareness of the metaphysical permanence of the heavens. Laozi took a different route, applying a cosmological view of metaphysical Dao as the source of all beings in the manifest world and holding ideal human values. Among humanity, Dao becomes the wellspring of all values, which implants the natural virtues of humaneness, responsibility, rites, and music through the mediation of virtuosity.

While reevaluating Daoist understanding of humaneness and responsibility, Laozi's views of rites and music also deserve reconsideration. The *Laozi* notes that "great music has no sound," showing the Daoist conception of music, on the level of Dao. This is significantly different from the Confucian focus on music as part of the rites in the political realm. A revised understanding of these features in Daoism is a worthy subject of further exploration.

To sum up, Laozi saw cosmic Dao and human life as operating in the same way and in line with one another, and therefore applied a general understanding of the workings of the cosmos to his philosophy of human life. This was a major breakthrough in ancient Chinese thought. In comparison, Confucian texts completely neglect discussions on ontological and cosmological levels, limiting their focus to the cultivation of ethical practice in society. This, not morality as such, represents the major difference between the two schools.

Chapter Four

Laozi's Thought

Chinese philosophers have consistently focused on human life and political thought. Discussions on these topics often include morality and ethics, pushing the scope of their thought to fit certain frameworks. A unique characteristic of Laozi's philosophy is that it breaks this mold and expands the scope of human thought from a focus on human life to looking at the entire cosmos. He examines a variety of human problems from both broad and focused perspectives. The philosophical system he develops extends discussions of the cosmos into the realm of human interaction, and then draws these concepts again from human interaction into politics. Understanding the true motivation behind Laozi's thought, it becomes clear that his "metaphysics" developed principally to serve as a foundation for understanding social interaction and politics (Xu 1963).

The moral aspects of Laozi's philosophy ground in the concept of Dao, in itself a fabrication. Through his personal experience in the world, Laozi was able to comprehend certain patterns or truths, which he then bundled together and called Dao. These patterns then became the characteristics or effects of Dao. At the same time, we can also understand Dao as something inherent to humans, something created to meet their needs and wants. Below, I introduce and interpret Laozi's moral thought, demonstrating how his metaphysics frame a humanistic and political philosophy.

Dimensions of Dao

Dao is the central concept of Laozi's thought—the presupposition around which his entire philosophical system develops. The *Laozi* describes Dao fairly consistently, but with several distinct connotations, sometimes described as many as six (Tang 1986). In some passages Dao is a metaphysical object; in other places, it is a pattern of the cosmos;

then again, it serves as the standard for human life—myriad forms of a single Dao. Let us look at these different meanings.

Laozi believes that Dao is an actual entity, and expresses this clearly in several passages. For example,

> Looking at it, it cannot be seen. It is called foreign.
> Listening to it, it cannot be heard. It is called silent.
> Grasping at it, it cannot be touched. It is called subtle.
> These three [aspects] cannot be examined,
> And thereby mix together to form one.
> The top is not bright, and the bottom is not dark.
> Continuous, it cannot be named.
> It then returns to [being] no thing.
> This is the form of no form,
> The outline of no thing.
> It is called "muddled" and "fleeting."
> Greeting it, its front cannot be seen.
> Following it, its back cannot be seen. (ch. 14)

Chapter 21, too, states that Dao is an entity that completely evades the five senses. The text further says,

> There is something mixed and complete,
> Originating before the heavens or the earth. . . .
> It is the mother of everything.
> I do not know its name.
> It could be called Dao,
> If forced to name it, I would call it great. (ch. 25)

In fact, calling it Dao is already a stretch for Laozi, since this is not its name but some conglomerate that has come together as one.

Why, then, can its name not be known? Because we cannot see or hear it. In other words, it is not a specific object with form or shape. The *Guanzi* says, "Things have certain forms, and forms have certain names" (37.2). Names come from form, and since Dao has no form, there is no way it can have a name.

This leads us to ask, why does Laozi say Dao is formless? What reason could he have for not wanting to name it? One reason is that anything that has form must be part of existence, a specific thing in space and time. Yet for Laozi Dao exists endlessly, so must be formless. Laozi repeatedly stresses that Dao cannot be named because named things are limited or restricted, but Dao is not. Generally, once something is given a name, it is defined as one thing, which distinguishes it from other things. "Jasmine," for example, once called "jasmine," cannot also be "rose." Dao is not delimited in this way, so cannot be described in language. The *Laozi* confirms this, "Dao that can be spoken of is not the constant Dao, the name that can be named is not the constant name" (ch. 1). Language cannot be used to talk about the "constant Dao," nor concepts used to express it. It is only referred to as Dao for the sake of convenience.

Although Dao is not a specific entity and is beyond our scope of knowledge, it is not simply an empty nothingness. *Laozi* 21 notes that Dao includes shapes, things, and essences. *Laozi* 25 describes Dao as exclusive and absolute within the cosmos (or as the cosmos), and that it is constant—i.e., it will never cease to exist. Changes of external things cannot cause Dao to fall out of existence, nor can external forces cause it to change. Dao is "independent and unchangeable" (ch. 25).

Some scholars have found Laozi's Dao comparable to Parmenides's "being," which seems appropriate, but is misleading. Although the Greek philosopher's concept is also singular, absolute, and permanent, it is fixed and static. Laozi's Dao is not set and unchanging; it is constantly shifting. Dao "moves in cycles and is never in danger [of being exhausted]" (ch. 25). It is a shifting and a moving thing. Constantly transforming, the cosmos shifts endlessly along with it; all beings follow Dao's movement and transformation. In this process, all beings come into and go out of existence, but Dao never leaves existence. What Laozi means by "unchangeable" when he says Dao is "independent and unchangeable" is that it never leaves existence. In fact, the movement of Dao produces all beings. This is the relationship between Dao and specific entities.

In the World

Laozi writes, "There is something mixed and complete, originating before the heavens and the earth" (ch. 25). Dao, as an entity, comes before the heavens and the earth: it creates them. Evidence for this proposal is found throughout the *Laozi*:

> Nonbeing is the name for the beginning of the heavens and earth; being is the name for the mother of all beings. (ch. 1)
>
> Dao is empty and cannot be filled through use. It is deep and mysterious like the forbear of all beings. (ch. 4)
>
> Everything in the world was born from being, and being was born from nonbeing. (ch. 40)

> Dao generates one, one generates two, two generates three, and three generates all beings. (ch. 42)
> Dao generates all beings, and virtuosity nourishes them. (ch. 51)

Dao is the origin of all beings in existence—the primordial natural force. It is full of endless potential and creative power. All life and growth that happen in the world are expressions of Dao. The endlessness of transformation, new life, and energy prove Dao's power.

Laozi describes the process of change from the cosmic singular Dao into various individual things as, "Dao generates one, one generates two, two generates three, and three generates all beings" (ch. 42). Each step brings Dao closer to becoming actual phenomena and creating the world. It cultivates and fosters them. Dao gives birth to all beings; it also is in all beings. Not limited by space or time, Dao comes before all beings and is unaffected by their changes. It is transcendent, but at the same time in all beings, cultivating and fostering them, and so is immanent as well.

The passages cited above from chapters 1 and 40 show more precisely what being and nonbeing mean as aspects of the larger concept of a cosmic Dao. They are opposite, but Laozi uses them in a way that shows that they are also connected. Nonbeing refers to limitlessness without any form or expression, and which includes limitless being. Indeed, nonbeing contains the infinite possibilities that may manifest in being. The immanence of the metaphysical Dao is how things are produced, which happens through the interplay of being and nonbeing.

Wang Bi argues that nonbeing is used to describe Dao's formlessness, while being indicates its form (which it takes on when producing things). Therefore, Laozi's "nonbeing" is not "nothing" or zero; it is a kind of hidden force. "Dao is hidden and nameless" (ch. 41). Ascribing the quality of being "hidden" to Dao articulates its formlessness, which is why we cannot perceive it. Our senses cannot experience it, and concepts cannot capture and describe it, so Laozi sometimes uses "nonbeing" as another name for Dao.[1]

Dao takes no form and cannot be seen; it is indeterminate and changing. However, it still expresses through phenomena a certain type of pattern or regularity that humans can follow. Laozi describes the

---

[1] Xu Fuguan writes, "The process of producing the world shows that Dao developed from having no form or quality to having form and quality" (1963: 337).

"way" of Dao by giving an account of how things in the world act, which provide us insight into Dao's movement.

One of the most striking characteristics of Dao is "reversal as the key movement of Dao" (ch. 40). Everything in nature, including living things and events, follow certain patterns. Reversal is one of the most constant of these. Things progress in a certain direction, but their development also returns them to their original state. "Reversal" can be understood as involving "complementarity" and "return."

Complementarity

Laozi thinks that all beings are formed from a situation where complementary opposites clash. He writes, "Being and nonbeing give birth to one another; difficulty and ease give birth to one another; long and short are comparable to one another; high and low exist in contrast to one another" (ch. 2). In human society, all values are also determined through complementary opposites. "Everything in the world knows the beauty of the beautiful, and thereby [the idea of] ugliness [is created]. Everything knows the good of good things, and thereby [the idea of] bad [is created]" (ch. 2).

This makes it clear that Laozi believes everything in the world has its complementary opposite, and that through the distinction of such opposition things come to be perceived. In other words, mutual creation through mutual opposition drives the development and transformation of all beings. He sees complementary opposites in all beings, including humans. "Misery—happiness is at its side. Happiness—misery is there too. Who can know the end of either?" (ch. 59). Even feelings are born from one another, giving rise to stories like the *Huainanzi*'s tale of the lost horse (13.20).

It shows how good fortune and bad luck are constantly reversed, one born out of the other, and thereby expresses their mutual interdependence. Most people think of the alternation of good fortune and bad luck as fate; they look for the good in the bad, or visa-versa. They all miss the deeper meaning. According to both the *Laozi* and *Huainanzi*, everything happy includes elements of misery, all misery has a grain of happiness. Some people develop bad habits or even encounter misfortune because they are lost in good feelings. Likewise, it is often only because someone has been very happy that they can become extremely sad or upset. Laozi concludes that happiness and misery in the world often shift into each other, and even include one another. Like everything else, they transform without end.

There are three major reasons why Laozi focuses on this issue. First, he sees worldly phenomena as having arisen through complementary evolution and contrast. When observing things, it is important to pay attention to both their positive and negative sides, since they never actually separate. This is the only way to understand something truly. In fact, according to Laozi, fully comprehending the positive or negative side of anything entails knowing its complementary opposite.

Second, Laozi points out the function of the negative side of things: it decisively shapes the entirety of objects, events, and states of affairs. Most people prefer to be first and of high rank, for example, but the *Laozi* reminds us not only that the low is the foundation for the high, but that it is actually more important. Nothing high could exist without the low. Most people also focus on possessing things, but Laozi insists that "being provides benefit while nonbeing provides the ability to function" (ch 11). Without nonbeing, anything present cannot be used.[2] The role of the negative side of things is therefore often more important than the positive.

Third, Laozi thinks that when something develops to its extreme, its primary state changes increasingly into its complementary opposite. "To weaken someone, first strengthen him. To crush someone, first praise him. To destroy someone, first allow him to rise. This is called 'hiding the light'" (ch. 36).[3] Here, developing a positive quality to an extreme leads to its opposite.[4] One can also look at the moon, which wanes when full and waxes once empty; or observe how the sky is darkest before dawn. Indeed, nature in general acts this way. Understanding that "things that prosper must also decline" can help one maintain a grasp on difficult situations and avoid disaster.

---

[2] Most people know that things present have a use, but they often overlook the fact that nonpresent things can be utilized as well. Laozi has many examples, like the empty space in a container, the empty hub of a wheel, or the emptiness of a room, to prove this point.

[3] "Hiding the light" is *weiming* 微明, also glossed by Wang Bi to mean "subtle understanding," and perhaps best understood as both.

[4] *Laozi* 36 may well be the most misunderstood chapter in the entire book. Many people think it speaks about some kind of trick or deceptive methods. Laozi simply shows that, if people act according to the pattern of "returning" and realize that all extremes entail their complementary opposite, they are likely to succeed.

Laozi has a lot to say about natural patterns of transformation and change. He writes, "The partial becomes complete; the warped becomes straight; the empty becomes full; the old becomes new" (ch. 22), and says, "Things may diminish, and thereby increase, or they many increase and thereby diminish" (ch. 42).

He furthermore reinforces the idea that this type of complementary transformation is a rule of the cosmos.

> Can the way of nature be compared to a bow?
> The high part is compressed [downward], the low part is lifted.
> Where there is abundance there will be loss,
> Deficiency will be compensated.
> The way of nature is taking from abundance
> To compensate for deficiency. (ch. 77)

That is to say, Laozi thinks that using abundance to supplement deficiency is an inherent pattern of nature. This also informs his idea of reversal, i.e., that things move and develop toward their complementary opposites. When things are in line with Dao, they follow such cyclical reversal as one of the key rules. Through patterns and concepts like this we gradually come closer to understanding Dao.

Cyclicality

Laozi also focuses on the circular movement of things as they change, understanding cyclicality in close relation to reversal. Not only do complementary opposites balance each other out, but they also move together in rhythmical cycles. This is another major characteristic of Dao.

> Emptiness brought to the extreme, stillness carefully guarded.
> All beings interact in their processes of activity,
> then I see them return [to their original state].
> Things that flourish all return to their roots.
>
> Going back to the roots is stillness,
> and this is called the fate of returning.
> Return to destiny is constant;
> Knowing what is constant is being bright.
> Not knowing what is constant
> [Leads to] sloppy actions and unfortunate deeds. (ch. 16)

> Something mixed and complete . . .
> Moving cyclically without beginning or end . . .
> If forced to name it, I would call it great.
> The great is flow, and flow is distance,
> And distance is reversal. (ch. 25)

Laozi says that Dao "moves cyclically without beginning or end," that it moves in a constant inexhaustible flow. Talking about this flow, he further explains Dao's cyclical movement and emphasizes that Dao is expansive, without boundaries, and that all beings come from Dao (ch. 25). Once things arise from primordial Dao and their cycles begin, they never leave Dao's patterns. Even being "far" only entails "reversal" or "returning," after which it all begins again.

Return also connotes cyclical movement (ch. 16). Looking at the natural world, Laozi concludes that everything follows a cyclical pattern. Each and every thing returns to its roots in the end. For Laozi, reversal means returning to the roots where something started, where the impetus for vitality is concentrated and existence renewed. That is what he means by, "Going back to the roots is stillness, and this is called "return to destiny" (ch. 16).

The metaphysical Dao is something that humans are unable to directly feel or cognize. Dao does exist, however, in the world, and it significantly influences our lives. Through its effects in the physical world, we begin to understand some of the characteristics of Dao, and thereby the metaphysical Dao actually enters into human life and provides guidance for our behavior. It becomes the model for how we should live, and how to order the world.

The metaphysical Dao that comes into the world and plays a role in human life can also be called virtuosity. Dao and virtuosity are two aspects of the same thing, Laozi uses the concepts "entity" and "use," respectively, to described their relationship. Virtuosity is how Dao is used, as well as its manifestation. The conglomerate Dao, in its acts of creation, internalizes itself into all beings and thereby forms their characteristics, which are called virtuosity. More simply put, Dao that becomes part of the world of experience is virtuosity. Its natural state, separate from human experience, we refer to as Dao, whereas the obvious features Dao takes on—the way we humans experience it and how we learn from it—can be called virtuosity. Virtuosity interacts with humans, and then returns back to the natural state of Dao.

This leads us to ask: What are the basic elements, or spirit, of Dao that humans are supposed to follow? Laozi believes that Dao is:

> self-so and acts non-assertively,
> the utmost void and guards stillness,
> generating [phenomena] but does not take [them] as its own,
> active but does not rely [on other things],
> nourishing [all beings] without controlling them,
> soft and weak,
> free from struggle,
> in the lowest position,
> in favor of [being the] last,
> loving,
> economical,
> simple.

All these are ways, in which Dao expresses its fundamental characteristics or spirit, the most central idea of which is "being self-so and non-assertive."

Practical Application

Chapters 1, 4, 21, 25, 32, 34, 42, and 51 give the best descriptions of Dao in terms of metaphysics, while others discuss it from the perspective of human life. Laozi connects these metaphysical descriptions with elements of phenomenal experience, proposing patterns of Dao as guides for human conduct that can help shape our approaches to personal and social issues. Laozi's abstract discussions of the metaphysical Dao thereby become highly pragmatic guides for human life. How, then, does Dao apply to social and political action?

Self-so

Self-so or "nature" (*ziran*) and non-assertive action (*wuwei*) are the most important concepts in Laozi's philosophy. To him, all phenomena should develop in accord with their own selves and fundamental states of being; they should not be restricted by external intention or will. Everything already possesses its own potential and ability; nothing from outside needs to be added. This is why Laozi uses the term "self-so"—an ideal of self actualization through a thing acting on its own accord, completely free of compulsion or interference.

Laozi's philosophy has also been called a philosophy of nature—a claim based largely on the line, "People follow the earth, the earth follows the heavens, the heavens follow Dao, and Dao follows *nature*" (ch. 25). In this sequence, not only does Dao follow nature, but all beings end up following it. When Laozi says that Dao follows nature, however, he actually means that Dao follows itself and not anything else. Dao relies on nothing but itself to determine its existence and movements. This being the case, understanding *ziran* as the natural world in this sentence is wrong; it is not a noun, and should be read as "self-so." It describes Dao following itself.

In fact, the term always connotes "self-so" in the *Laozi*. Passages in chapters 17, 23, 51 and 64, use it in ways that cannot be understood as referring to the natural world, but rather indicate things following their own intrinsic dispositions. For example, Laozi writes, "[In antiquity, when people followed Dao,] success in their work led the people to say 'we are self-so'" (ch. 17). They said this because their accomplishment came about without awareness of any political power. The government made itself responsible for supporting the people, not controlling or disturbing them, and people believed their achievements were due to themselves alone. Here, Laozi is arguing that when people are not aware of government intervention, they become free and happy, and society is well ordered.

He also says, "Being sparse with words is self-so. A strong wind does not last for more than one morning, and rain one day" (ch. 23). Here, "sparse with words" means not excessively instructing or commanding people. Speaking little is an ideal for rulers and officials, related to Laozi's proposition that one can "teach without words" (ch. 43). The more the government interferes with people's lives, the worse things become, because people are no longer acting of their own accord (ch. 17). If this rule is not followed, then, like a strong wind or heavy rain, ruling power will be short lived.

Likewise, it is precisely because Dao and virtuosity do not intrude on people's lives that everyone praises them. All beings in the world honor Dao and virtuosity, and that they do so not by decree by rather of their own accord—that is, naturally self-so (ch. 51).

Finally, Laozi relates this idea to sages. "Sages desire what other people do not desire, and do not value rare things. They study what others do not study, and return to what most people pass over. They help things develop according to their own self-so and do not dare to act assertively" (ch. 64). Like officials who are supposed to be passive, the sage simply allows things to act according to their natural tendencies. This is also the same way Dao supports things—by not interfering. Following their own courses, everything acts naturally, in line with their own individual natures rather than some larger nature that is somehow other or separate.

According to these passages, Laozi's self-so aims at dispelling the influence of outside agents, whose interference is harmful for individual things and their development. Importantly, "the heavens and earth are not humane, and take all beings as straw dogs" (ch. 5). That is, the universe has no favorites, nor is it selfish; it allows things to promote themselves. The sage also acts in this manner, respecting the way the world works and allowing the people to flourish self-so. This is done by adopting a mode of being described as non-assertive action, how humans model the behavior of Dao. In other words, the term "self-so" applies generally to the natural courses of phenomena in the world, while non-assertive action describes a manner of human conduct. The two words, however, essentially refer to the same concept.

Non-Assertive Action

Non-assertive action is central to Laozi's thought and very close to self-so. Textual evidence for this claim is as follows, "Dao is consistent in acting in non-assertive action, and thus there is nothing that is not done" (ch. 37). Dao moves in accordance with the intrinsic qualities of each being, which is how the metaphysical interacts with the world of experience. This is, however, the only time Laozi uses discusses Dao in terms of non-assertive action—the terms generally describes a concept reserved for politics and is typically used to denounce those who think that assertive action (*youwei* 有为) is necessary for ruling.[5]

Assertive action is how rulers exercise power to promote their own personal interests or desires. Laozi thinks that this type of selfishness is responsible for many social problems. "In the world, the more prohibitions, the greater the people's poverty. . . . The more laws are made and displayed, the more robbers and thieves there will be" (ch. 57). Similarly, "The people starve because of the taxes the rulers gobble up, causing

---

[5] Hu Shi claims that Laozi is opposed to assertive action in politics mainly as a reaction to the corrupt governments of his day. "All advocacy of non-assertive action in political philosophy," he states, "is in reaction to overbearing government policies" (1989).

famine. The rulers struggle to govern because they take assertive action, making their leadership ineffective" (ch. 75). Excessive prohibitions leave the people at a loss what to do, and overly strict laws create hardship for the people. Harsh punishment and abuse, as well as heavy taxes feeding greed, bring destitution upon the people.

Laozi saw the widespread hardship caused by heavy taxation first-hand. As the government centralized power, turning authoritarian, the lives of common people became increasingly unstable. The government that should have served the people became, instead, oppressive. Laozi expounds, "Those who wear elegant clothing, carry sharp swords, indulge in eating, and have an overabundance of things—these [rulers] are robbers and show-offs. They do not accord with Dao" (ch. 53). Dao wants nothing to do with luxury or showing off. When rulers harm the people, and bolster their own desires to live in extravagance, the people's fields turn to dust and the granaries empty. This is what Laozi calls "not according with Dao."

If this type of situation goes on unrectified, Laozi predicts even worse calamities. "If the people do not fear authority, then even greater misfortune will befall them" (ch. 72). When rulers and officials are oppressive, an extreme will eventually be reached, and from there things will begin to reverse. He continues, "When the people do not fear death, how can they be threatened with death?" (ch. 74). In other words, if people are continually mistreated, they will come to care little for their own lives, in which case not even the death penalty can be used to keep them in line.

These arguments are the result of Laozi's reflections on the politics of his day. He saw rulers and officials who acted in impetuous ways that often far exceeded their capacities and caused calamity for their states. It is against this background that Laozi came to advocate non-assertive action, which he saw as the only possible solution. We can even say that developing a theory of non-assertive action was the very motivation for and goal of his book, and even composes the foundation of his metaphysics. Laozi writes:

> I act non-assertively, and the people transform themselves;
> I love stillness, and the people correct themselves;
> I do not manage things, and the people become rich of themselves;
> I am free of desires, and the people become simple of themselves. (ch. 57)

Here "loving stillness," "not managing things," and "being free of desires" are all descriptions of non-assertive action. "Loving stillness" is directed at rulers and officials who cause clamor and disrupt things. "Not managing things" is a critique of those who are strict and cruel in creating or carrying out policies. The biggest problem, that of selfishness, he opposes with the admonition to "be free of desires." If the government embodies these principles and acts non-assertively, then the people will improve themselves. They will be able to develop naturally self-so into a stable, peaceful, and rich society.

Advocating non-assertive action produces an attitude of noninterference that gives the world a great amount of freedom. Selfish rulers and officials act precisely opposite this, putting their hands in everything and thereby negatively affecting people's lives by taking away their freedom and security. Promoting non-assertive action is an attempt to dispel this problem. Although Laozi is not building a democratic society, he hopes for freedom.

Laozi's non-assertive action does not mean doing nothing; it means acting appropriately and effectively. People often misread non-assertive action, especially misunderstanding the idea that by non-assertive action there is nothing one cannot do (based on ch. 37), and believing it suggests that one hide the appearance of action and work in secret. This makes Laozi look like some sort of schemer (e.g., Qian 2005), which is entirely inaccurate. He says nothing to suggest that he endorses such behavior.

This misinterpretation is based on an overall misunderstanding of Laozi's philosophy. The line about non-assertive action actually means that, as long as one acts appropriately, anything can be accomplished. Non-assertive action is by no means furtive. Rather, it is a method one adopts to take effective action. Laozi wants people to act with the right attitude and in the right way. He praises Dao as "acting but not relying [on other things]," (ch. 2) and even closes the *Laozi* by noting that sages "act without struggling [against the situation]" (ch. 81). He motivates people to action, and even to help themselves, but not by means of being controlling, relying too heavily on others, coercion, or creating conflict. One should not act selfishly or greedily.

Emptiness and Stillness

Laozi writes, "Emptiness brought to extreme, stillness carefully guarded" (ch. 16)—this is the primordial state of all beings. Faced with a chaotic world, full of disputes and war, he wants to promote emptiness and stillness as alternative models for human action and affairs.

Sima Tan, in his work *Lun liujia yaozhi* 论六家要旨 (The Arguments of Six Schools), argues that Daoist thought is based on the concept of emptiness. Laozi writes, "Dao is empty, and cannot be filled through use. It is deep and mysterious like the forbearer of all beings" (ch. 4). The emptiness or void nature of Dao is the origin of all beings—an endless source that generates phenomena and assists in their development. Laozi also writes, "Can the space between the heavens and the earth be compared to bellows?" (ch. 5) The bellows symbolizes a functional but empty state. The space between the heavens and the earth is empty, but its use is endless. As soon as movement begins, empty space becomes invaluable—essential to creation—and because it is empty, it can never be used up. Think of a valley. Contrasted with the hills or mountains that surround it, it is quite "empty"; yet this is where water flows and life flourishes. Laozi specifically uses the image "the higher virtuosity is like a valley" (ch. 41) to describe the mental state of someone exceptional.

Laozi's valley of emptiness can be contrasted with its opposite—fullness. Fullness in turn expresses "being full of one's self," which is exactly what leads to corruption. "One who displays himself is not bright; one who thinks himself right is not distinguished; one who shows-off will not succeed; one who is conceited does not grow" (ch. 24). This reminds people not to think too highly of themselves.

Things that are empty, like people who are not full of themselves, are necessarily still or quiet. "All beings interact in their processes of activity, then I see them return [to their original state]. Things that flourish all return back to their roots. Going back to roots is stillness, and this is called the return to destiny" (ch. 16). Things grow, and Laozi notices that they follow a cyclical pattern as they develop. That is, there are many different states of being, yet it is the final state of stillness that all beings eventually return to—and where they began, as well. Laozi wants people to be aware of this natural phenomenon so that they may reflect it in society and politics.

Laozi is especially interested in having rulers and officials make use of stillness in their lives and policies. "Clarity and stillness make everything correct" (ch. 45). The effect of clarity and stillness could not be greater. He approaches this from a different angle, as well, saying, "Without desires, using stillness, everything in the world sets itself [right]" (ch. 45). If one is not bothered by intense desires, one can reach a pure and quiet state. As cited above, Laozi would have rulers recite the lines, "I love stillness, and the people correct themselves; . . . I am free of desires, and the people become simple of themselves" (ch. 57)

Clearly, being free of desires relates closely to clarity and stillness. Above we saw that acting in non-assertive action allows people to become simple and set themselves right. Saying that "I am free of desires, and the people will become simple themselves" is another way of showing that desires oppose simplicity. Laozi, however, is not talking about all desires; he is attacking devious, bad desires, not basic human desires or needs. If only rulers and officials were able to control their excessive desires, then society could become stable and safe.

The opposite of stillness is being upset, anxious or annoyed. As Laozi puts it ,

> Heaviness is the root of lightness;
> Stillness is the ruler of excitement.
> The sage may walk all day,
> But he remains close to his baggage [wagons].
> Although there are beautiful scenes,
> He does not depart [from his route].
> How does one who has thousands of chariots [extreme wealth]
> [Preserve] his body and take the world lightly?
> Acting frivolously, one loses the roots;
> Acting impetuously, one loses ascendancy. (ch. 26)

Stillness and heaviness or solemnity are thus related to one another. Keeping one means preserving the other, so Laozi praises both. He thinks that a ruler, in his daily life, must be mindful of stillness and heaviness. Even if a ruler can live a luxurious and pleasurable life, in order to be calm and tranquil, stillness and heaviness are required. Anxious and excited behavior on the ruler's part is often abusive and dangerous for the people. Laozi decries this when he writes, "Governing a large state is like frying a small fish" (ch. 60). When frying a small fish, one should be careful not to turn it over too much, or else it will fall apart. Controlling a state similarly requires rulers to keep things pure and simple, and not institute heavy punishments or complicated laws.

Laozi's conception of stillness has a specific background. First, he saw the rulers of his time acting without restraint, pursuing bodily pleasures. He warns, "The five [i.e. all] colors make people's eyes blind; the five notes make people's ears deaf, the five flavors make people's mouth's lose their sense of taste. Wild chariot hunting expeditions make people's heart-and-mind's crazy" (ch. 12). In other words, reigning in one's desires and the excessive distractions they lead to is necessary to experience the world with clarity. Second, Laozi attacks the way he saw rulers abuse their people, especially through heavy taxation and brutal punishments. Only calm and pure leadership allows the people to feel secure, which is a requisite for the securing of political stability.

These arguments further operate on an additional personal level. Laozi wants each individual to strive to become pure and calm. One should be able to remain clear even when busy, and compose oneself when anxious. Being still does not mean not moving, but rather preserving mental and emotional clarity while moving. Not dissimilar to the dynamics of non-assertive action, for Laozi there is movement in stillness and stillness in movement.

Soft and Weak

Reversing more common ideas of power, Laozi writes, "Dao uses weakness" (ch. 40), and, "[Dao] exists continuously but indistinctly, and accords not with specific purpose" (ch. 6). Laozi describes Dao's method of creation as soft and weak, yet nevertheless continuous and unending. Dao's use of weakness can be understood as analogous to non-assertive action. Precisely because of the delicacy with which Dao performs, things do not seem created by an external force, but rather born of themselves.

In the human realm, weakness is also beneficial. Laozi claims, "The soft and weak overcome the hard and strong" (ch. 36). Laozi finds evidence for this throughout the natural world:

> When humans are born, they are soft and weak,
> When they die, they are hard and strong.
> All beings [are like this].
> Grass and trees are born soft and brittle,
> When they die they are dry and withered.
> So the hard and strong are followers of death,
> And the soft and weak are followers of life. (ch. 76)

In the world of experience, things that are hard and strong are often dead, whereas living things are generally soft and weak or pliable. Laozi uses human beings as an example. The human body is soft and weak when alive, but just few hours after death it turns stiff and inflexible. Grass and trees are the same, as are most other things in the world. This is why Laozi concludes that it is preferable to promote the soft and weak.

Additionally, strength and sturdiness even seem to invite disaster. Tall trees attract lumberjacks and are more likely to be toppled by a strong storm, whereas smaller trees, grass and weeds, being soft and weak, both fail to entice their own death and simply sway with the wind. Moreover, water, which Laozi considers the softest of things, can quite simply never be cut or damaged. Laozi thereby takes water as a central image in his writings:

> There is nothing softer or weaker than water.
> Yet, nothing hard or strong can be used to attack it.
> here is nothing that resists change.
> The weak overcomes the strong,
> And the soft overcomes the hard.
> There is no one who does not know this,
> And there is no one who is able to act accordingly. (ch. 78)

Laozi also argues, "The softest thing in the world hits against the hardest thing in the world [and harms it]" (ch. 43). In other words, water is the softest thing in the world, and proves astoundingly effective in attacking strong and hard things. Even small drops of water, if persistent, will eventually erode a rock. Floods can ruin a field and bring down the strongest pillars. The firm and study cannot stand up to water. Laozi sees water's exemplary "weakness" as providing it indomitability.

This point aims at those who advocate the use of strength. These people are often selfish, pompous, full of themselves, and according to Laozi bring about most of the world's struggle and strife. This brings us to another pair of Laozi's major points: "not struggling and downward conduct. Not struggling (*buzheng* 不争) focuses on the unobstructed efficacy of proper action, while downward conduct (*chuxia* 处下) champions the power of the soft and weak and involves elements of modesty, prudence, and broadmindedness.

Water is also central to the *Laozi* as an analogy for these points. In addition to being soft and weak, water gathers in low places—conducts itself downward—does not struggle, and benefits the people. Laozi thinks that people should try to reflect these properties in their own lives.

Downward conduct is a manner of being effective through softness and weakness, and connotes humility. Laozi often uses water analogies to express this point, describing how rivers not only flow downward but also eventually feed into lakes or oceans. He aims to show the advantages of such downward movement over people's all to common struggle to move upwards. To Laozi, Dao is found in "rivers, streams and lakes, oceans" (ch. 32). He believes that if more people came to appreciate downward movement then they would be less inclined to disagree and fight with one another. The idea of not struggling is based on this view.

In society, people constantly struggle with one another as they seek ways to benefit themselves. As an alternative to this, Laozi proposes the ideal of water as "benefiting things without struggling" (ch. 8), and the way of the sage as "acting without struggling" (ch. 81). He does not mean that people should give up on the fulfillment of their personal needs or ignore society and become hermits. Laozi advocates acting in ways that are beneficial to the surrounding world and all the people in it. The goal is to balance out social inequalities, which otherwise foster more conflict and struggle, through not struggling—that is, acting in a self-so manner that benefits all of humankind, not just oneself. This kind of benevolent action champions the avoidance of conflict and strife over the achievement of success or fame, and is a lofty ethic not easily realized. When Laozi advocates "not reveling in one's accomplishments" (ch. 2), "not claiming success" (ch. 34), and "withdrawing to the way of the heavens" (ch. 34), he is talking about not struggling. It is all about lessening human conflict.

Evaluation

Laozi's philosophical system starts with Dao. He argues that it is the beginning of heaven and earth and the mother of all beings; yet, all of this is outside experience. Dao is not something that can be known through sensory perception; it is the pattern on which human life is modeled, and following it can solve human problems. Its actual existence can be neither proven nor denied. In this sense, we may liken Dao to the political presupposition that "everyone is created equal." Are we all truly created equal? We cannot corroborate this foundational assumption's empirical veracity, nor can we fully disprove it. Laozi's Dao can be known from a "hypothetical viewpoint," but not an "existential" one.[6]

---

[6] The author glosses his Chinese terms *jiashe de guandian* 设定的观点 and *cunzai de guandian* 存在的观点, here with the English terms "hypothetical viewpoint" and "existential viewpoint." The latter likely refers to a viewpoint from within existence, i.e. an experiential or empirical viewpoint.

The development of Laozi's Dao can also be said to come from innate human feeling. Laozi wants to find something stable in a world of change—something beyond the individual—to enrich the human spirit and give people a connection to the cosmos.

Some scholars have argued that Laozi's metaphysical Dao is just an attempt at satisfying natural human interest in philosophical concepts. This interest, however, is precisely what has opened our thinking and understanding to be able to come to a clearer view of the world around us.

Moreover, Laozi's theory of the origin of the cosmos is extremely important in the history of Chinese thought. Positing Dao as the originator of things breaks away from the old legends of gods creating the world. Laozi says that Dao "seems to be before gods" (ch. 4). He leaves no place for gods (or a God), as we saw in above from the forty-second chapter; all beings follow Dao, or self-so patterns, which means that there is no creator to emulate. Even the line, "The heavens and earth are not humaneness, and take all beings as straw dogs" (ch. 5), expresses a creatorless understanding of the cosmos that sits in direct opposition to ancient Chinese superstitions and their restrictions on human behavior.

When Laozi speaks of the heavens (*tian*), he is talking about what naturally arises from Dao, not about any higher force(s) possessing will or intention. The heavens are not an ultimate power, and people cannot upset them (as opposed to traditional beliefs). Laozi's theory thus proposes that each thing develop along its own path, or according to its own self. The historical influence of this thought proves his metaphysics extremely useful.

When Dao comes into the human world it expresses certain patterns, the implications of which for humans are clear. These patterns include "self-so and non-assertive action," "emptiness and stillness," "softness and weakness," "not struggling," and "downward conduct." These characteristic tendencies of Dao can be found throughout the manifest world. By introducing these ideas, Laozi's hopes to create a more harmonious society. His society, like every society in the world, was full of both hidden and apparent conflict, the most obvious example of which is war. The *Laozi* explicitly and repeatedly denounces war; however, it does caution that war can be unavoidable, and one must nevertheless prepare oneself to face it if necessary (see ch. 31).

We can thereby see that Laozi had many goals in writing his classic; and yet if one looks at just one or two aspects of his thought he is easily misinterpreted. Scholars have argued that Laozi's thought is negative, pessimistic, or advocates ignoring society and becoming a hermit. These are all gross misreadings of the *Laozi.* As shown above, he is very much interested in society, and especially politics. Truly, he does condemn taking credit for achievements, seeking personal gain, or striving for fame, but that is because he sees people behaving viciously and hurting one another when they engage in such behavior. He wants people to make great achievements, but not at the price of harming others. People should help one another and contribute to society, which is a positive and optimistic way to integrate oneself into humanity.

Laozi's advocacy of "emptiness and stillness" is both critical of and illuminating for how we live our lives. Remaining empty and still is an emotional and mental state that preserves psychological focus. Only this type of mentality can cultivate a genuine, simple and wise person. If we look at the way people are today, anxious, busy and always in a rush, we can understand why deep thinking and reflection are difficult. Laozi wants people to be attentive to their inner states, and cultivate themselves properly—an especially meaningful message in the modern world.

Ontology and Experience

In the 6th century BCE, at the end of the Spring and Autumn period, Kongzi redefined the Zhou dynasty patriarchal ethic, which went on to become the foundation of Chinese culture. At the same time, Laozi developed a system of thought unlike any other before, thereby beginning Chinese philosophy. Dao is the core concept of Laozi's philosophy. It is the origin of all beings, the ontological beginning and shaper of human values.

Laozi was the first thinker in China to make being and nonbeing into philosophical concepts. The two concepts interact dynamically as aspects of Dao; they have been interpreted variously over the course of history. The transmitted *Laozi* contains two important but conflicting arguments about them. First it says that "being and nonbeing give birth to one another" (ch. 2), then it states that "being is born from nonbeing" (ch. 40). Laozi thereby raises the two to the highest ontological categories, while also making them essential facets of his cosmology.

Before Laozi, most thinkers concentrated on entities in the world. Laozi shifted that focus to Dao, providing a systematic theoretical explanation of all phenomena of the existence. He uses being and nonbeing in different ways, metaphysically and ontologically or in their everyday sense in the world of experience. This has caused a great deal of misunderstanding in subsequent studies. In order to properly understand what Laozi means, we must first clarify the difference between being and nonbeing in the ontological-metaphysical sense, i.e., as they relate to Dao, and then distinguish them in their meaning within the world of experience.

Laozi first describes present and nonpresent as aspects of the origin of all beings. "Nonbeing is the name for the beginning of the heavens and the earth; being is the name for the mother of all beings" (ch. 1). Dao itself is without form or limit, and can thus be called "nonbeing;" yet it also exists, and so is "being" as well.

Then again he uses the terms in the everyday sense as elements of the phenomenal world.

> Thirty spokes unite in one place—
> The nonbeing [in their hub] makes the cart's use present.
> Clay is made into vessels—
> The nonbeing [in their middle] makes the vessels' use present.
> Doors and windows are cut to make a house—
> The nonbeing [in their walls] makes the house's use present.
> Therefore,
> Being provides benefits,
> Nonbeing provides the ability to function. (ch. 11)

Here Laozi illustrates the dynamic of being and nonbeing in worldly phenomena, highlighting their mutual interdependence—the same relationship they have in their metaphysical sense.

Laozi's discussion of movement (*dong* 动) and stillness (*jing* 静), too, exhibits these two levels, the ontological-metaphysical and the world of experience. In the former sense, when talking about Dao as an entity, Laozi says that it is continuously moving. He explains, "Returning is the movement of Dao" (ch. 40); Dao "moves in cycles and is never in danger [of being exhausted]" (ch. 25). Dao's movement is constant and part of the foundation of all beings, which is why they also move continuously. "Return to destiny is constant" (ch. 16), which highlights Dao's constancy as well as its continuous movement and the cyclical nature of that movement.

Let us not forget, however, that "going back to roots is stillness, and this is called return to destiny" (ch. 16). These characteristics of Dao foreshadow the mutually complementary nature of movement and stillness that characterizes Laozi's view of worldly phenomena. The line, "Who can rest in amid turbidity to create clarity? Who can rouse amid stillness to generate vitality?" (ch. 15), therefore, describes stillness within Dao's constant movement, which Laozi considers also characteristic of efficacious movement within the human realm. Huang-Lao Daoists in particular went on to embrace this concept.

Speaking more specifically to the world of experience, Laozi describes the manifest world, "Empty, it is not exhausted; moving, more comes out" (ch. 5), reminding us that things constantly move through empty space. As Laozi lived in troubled times, however, he champions stillness in society and politics over (excessive) movement. He writes, "Purity and stillness make everything correct" (ch. 46), and says, "Acting frivolously, one loses his roots; Acting impetuously, one loses his ascendancy" (ch. 26). The emphasis on stillness can be traced to the *Yijing*. Through Laozi, it became an influential caution against rash or impulsive action for later rulers as well as a fundamental element of Neo-Confucian thought.

Sima Tan talks about Laozi and Zhuangzi being skilled at taking emptiness as the "root" and using things accordingly. He sets the term "root" (*ben* 本) in a dichotomous relationship with "function" (*yong* 用), and later Wang Bi establishes a similar relationship between "substance" (*ti* 体) and "function." The "emptiness" (*xuwu* 虚无) Sima Tan mentions is what Zhuangzi calls the "root" (*ben'gen* 本根), i.e., an analogy for Dao. Sima's "using things accordingly" is based the *Laozi*, "Dao is empty, and when used cannot not be filled" (ch. 4). Here Laozi argues that Dao is endlessly useful, precisely because it is empty and thus inexhaustible. In fact Laozi talks implicitly of Dao's substance and function throughout. In terms of function, for example, he notes that "Dao uses weakness" (ch. 40). In a statement of both Dao's substance and function, we moreover find, "Great fullness is like a void, its use is inexhaustible" (ch. 45). In addition to discussing these aspects of Dao, Laozi also talks about substance and function in the phenomenal world, as noted earlier.

While Laozi implicitly discusses substance and function, the two became major philosophical concepts in their own right in Wang Bi's commentary. He picked up on Laozi's use of these ideas and explicated a philosophy in which nonbeing (Dao) is "substance" and being (phenomena) is "function." Wang argues that everything in the world functions through nonbeing, while simultaneously also finding substance through it. These developments of Laozi's thought were not only pivotal for the Dark Learning movement in Wang Bi's time but also significantly impacted the development of Buddhist thought in China and eventually

Neo-Confucianism. Centuries of discourse on substance and function can in fact be traced to Wang Bi interpretation of Laozi.

Being and nonbeing, movement and stillness, and substance and function are Daoist concepts that are both essentially metaphysical and also resound throughout the phenomenal world. In the world of experience, being and nonbeing are mutually generative, arising through each other—an understanding that embodies Laozi's theory that interchanging opposites complete one another. On the level of Dao, being and nonbeing are complementary qualities that allow it to be immanent yet at the same time limitless and without form.

When describing Dao, Laozi says that in movement there is stillness. In the world of experience movement and stillness can be used to cultivate one another, but Laozi would have people, especially rulers and officials, be partial toward stillness, and cautions again rash actions. Laozi only brings up the concepts of substance and function indirectly, but Wang Bi's commentary turned these implicit ideas and their relationship into major philosophical topics that have been explored by diverse schools of Chinese thought ever since.

Chapter Five

Laozi and Pre-Qin Philosophy

The direct successors of the *Laozi* are the schools of Yang Zhu, Liezi, and Zhuangzi. The text influenced the overall culture of the state of Qi and inspired the thought of the Jixia Academy, the largest school of the Warring States period. Dominantly Daoist, Jixia thought yet also integrated the ideas of other thinkers and strongly influenced Mengzi's cosmology and Xunzi's epistemology as well as his vision of nature. The *Guanzi* and Jixia thought intersect at many points, both using Laozi to develop theories of politics and economy.

Many scholars in China argue that the Jixia and Guanzi schools share certain characteristics with Huang-Lao Daoism, claimed to have originated in the state of Qi and spread to Chu. This makes it difficult to distinguish the traditions begun by the Jixia thinkers from Qi and the Huang-Lao school from Chu. However, since the excavation of the *Huangdi sijing* at Mawangdui in 1973 a much better understanding of Huang-Lao Daoism has been possible. We also know that Laozi's thought traveled west, as it plays a crucial role in Han Feizi's philosophy and in the *Lüshi chunqiu*, associated with the state of Qin.

Toward the end of the Spring and Autumn period, when Lao Dan lived, many famous hermits appeared. As recorded in the *Lunyu*, Confucians associated them with Daoists. Some of them espoused ideas similar to those of Lao Dan, which is not surprising, since once Lao Dan's *Laozi* became known, it spread very quickly. However, this does not make them truly Daoist. Essentially every Chinese thinker since his time has borrow his ideas to a greater or lesser degree. Still, there are four major schools claiming to be direct followers of the *Laozi*: mainstream Daoism, the Jixia school, Huang-Lao, and the *Yizhuan* tradition. Let us look at these in turn.

Mainstream Daoism

Yang Zhu, Liezi, and Zhuangzi are the most representative figures of Daoism after Lao Dan. They followed the *Laozi* in making Dao, emptiness, self-so, and non-assertive action the core of their philosophies. Yang Zhu and Liezi probably lived at the beginning of the Warring States Period, slightly before Zhuangzi. They were, moreover, preceded by a few direct inheritors of Laozi's thought.

The first of them was Guan Yin 关尹, originally from the state of Qin, born shortly after Lao Dan. In the "Tianxia" 天下 chapter of the *Zhuangzi*, the two are praised as "genuine sages of antiquity" (33.5). The *Hanshu* also records the *Guanyinzi* 关尹子 (Book of Master Guan Yin) as a Daoist text, although unfortunately lost today and an earlier text, thought to be authentic, proven fake.[1] We know from the *Zhuangzi* that Guan Yin shared many of the same ideas as Laozi. Among these were seeing Dao as the root of all beings and praising modesty and humility, weakness and emptiness. The *Zhuangzi* mentions that Guan Yin had his own unique ideas as well and appears to have concerned himself principally with the "heart-and-mind," making his greatest contributions in this area. Guan Yin's impact on Zhuangzi and other thinkers of pre-Qin Daoist philosophy is quite clear.

Gengsang Chu and Wenzi

Gengsang Chu is mentioned in both the *Liezi* and *Zhuangzi* as having a thorough comprehension of Laozi's teachings. Cheng Xuanying's 成玄英 (7th c. CE) commentary to the *Zhuangzi* also claims that he was the brightest of all Laozi's students. Sadly, none of his works, or even records of them, have survived, so it is impossible to know anything about his thought. The *Kangcangzi* 亢仓子 (Book of Master Kangcang), which claims to reconstruct his philosophy, came into being approximately a millennium after his death.

Wenzi 文子 was another student of Laozi. He lived around the same time as Kongzi. The *Hanshu* notes that the text *Wenzi* consisted of nine chapters; the *Suishu* 隋书 (History of the Sui Dynasty) as well as

[1] Jiang Guobao (2009) argues that ontological ideas in the *Guanyinzi*, such as coupling Dao and *qi*, and synthesizing the heart-and-mind, human tendencies and emotions, began in the Song dynasty, so today's version of the *Guanyinzi* must be post-Song.

both the *Xin* 新 and *Jiu Tangshu* 旧唐书 (New and Old Histories of the Tang) have it as consisting of twelve sections, matching the groupings in extant versions. There has been some suspicion regarding the authenticity of the *Wenzi*, but so far no decisive consensus.

Throughout the *Wenzi*, King Ping of Chu 楚平王 engages in dialogue with Wenzi about Dao. At one point, it says: "King Ping asks Wenzi, 'I have heard that you know Lao Dan's Dao'" (3.20), showing him as a disciple of Laozi. There are also many attempts to explain and develop Laozi's ideas in the *Wenzi*, which frequently comments directly on the *Laozi*. Like Laozi, Wenzi argues that Dao is the origin of the heavens and the earth, without form or shape, and yet pervasive throughout the cosmos, both in its manifestation as phenomena and as universal patterns. This text furthermore appears to have been instrumental in the founding of the Jixia Academy.

Wenzi's thought also includes Confucian, Mohist, and Legalist ideas, which he expresses in his discussions of morality, rites, and wisdom. Laozi wants to exclude humaneness, responsibility, the rites, and wisdom from morality, but Wenzi includes them. He states, "Ancient sages who understood Dao [could be classified thus:] those who understood deeply were called Dao and virtuosity; those who understood somewhat were called humane and responsible; and those who understood superficially were called ritually appropriate and wise" (3.13). Here we find Dao and virtuosity, humaneness and responsibility, and rites and wisdom broken down into hierarchical categories. They are all, however, included within Dao.

Wenzi's conceptions of humaneness and the rites are not entirely Confucian. He says that humaneness is "caring for others without being selfish" (3.3), which is more like Mozi. His definition of the rites is to "be yielding and keep to the soft, being female to the world" (3.11.3).

> In those who follow the rites, polish their natural tendencies, and correct their feelings, the eyes may desire [to look at something], but they are prevented from transgressing what is appropriate. Their heart-and-mind may be happy, but it is kept in check by the rites. . . . The rites cannot prevent or rid people of desires, but can control them. (*Wenzi* 10.4)

Wenzi argues that the rites help to control people's feelings and actions, which pushes the concept closer to that of the law, developed famously by Xunzi at the Jixia Academy.

When King Ping of Chu asks Wenzi how the laws came into being, he responds, "Leaders created laws. They did so by first self-examining, creating laws able to govern themselves, which would then succeed in governing the people" (7.13). Wenzi posits that laws serve to keep rulers in line and prevent them from making arbitrary decisions, thus failing to use their power in the manner necessitated by their role. This type of democratic, anti-tyrannical ideal appears also in the *Laozi* and *Zhuangzi*.

Wenzi also agrees with these two Daoist thinkers that everything has its own "perspective." His emphasis on individual uniqueness and opposition to assembly-line standardization is especially close to the *Zhuangzi*.

In some ways, Wenzi strongly agrees with Laozi's praise of softness, but he also adds ideas of creating hardness out of softness and points out that the two each have their own pros and cons. He cautions that one should not be too partial to either. "The sage should be yin or yang, soft or hard, weak or strong, and move or be still depending on the times, and contribute according to the situation" (5.1). Wenzi was able to recognize that success is largely dependent on objective factors, such as timing and the particulars of a situation. Like Laozi, he decries cunning and subversive plots as well as militarism.

In sum, although the *Wenzi* clearly makes important contributions to Daoist thought, it was composed after the *Liezi* and *Zhuangzi*, and mostly represents the thought of earlier Daoist thinking. It principally diverges from earlier Daoist works in promoting of the power of the masses and supporting Mohist and Legalist ideas. The same influence is also evident in the *Huainanzi*, which includes three quarters of the present-day *Wenzi* (see Ding 2009).

Yang Zhu

Yang Zhu, aka Yangzi 杨子, was born in the ancient state of Wei, present-day Henan. Neither the *Shiji* nor the *Hanshu* contain any record of his life. The *Liezi*, however, devotes an entire chapter to him, from which we can understand his thought. Many pre-Qin thinkers, including Mengzi, classify Yang Zhu alongside Mozi, proving his importance as an early Warring States thinker.

Yang Zhu's thought has often been misinterpreted as advocating selfishness, starting with Mengzi's criticism. Mengzi's attack on Yang, however, not only misrepresents him, it also proves his irrational disapproval for anyone with a different viewpoint. In fact, looking at the various pre-Qin thinkers' remarks about Yang Zhu, it becomes clear that his most central idea is "valuing life over things."

Thus, Han Feizi writes that Yang, "even for the sake of gaining the best benefit in the whole world, would not pull a hair [from his body]. Rulers should follow this, and consider it proper, respecting Yang's intention and action, valuing life over things" (50.4). The *Lüshi chunqiu* comments, "Yang valued himself" (17.7), while the *Huainanzi* notes, "With his entire nature he protected what was genuine; he would not tire his form over things. This was Yangzi's position" (13.12).

From these records it is clear that Yang Zhu valued his life and body very highly, and would not risk harming either for the sake of material objects. This perspective is not unlike Laozi's own. Additionally, valuing oneself serves as a way of respecting individual life; it is an expression of the Daoist admiration for nature, especially as Daoist thought regards nature as something individual.

The later school of thought that followed Yang Zhu further developed the master's basic respect for the individual. The best record of this is the "Yang Zhu" chapter in the *Liezi* (ch. 7). It has, "The ancients would not harm themselves in the slightest to benefit the world. . . . If everyone refrained from harm, refrained from benefiting the world, the world would be well ordered" (7.11). When viewed alongside the citations above, we find that this is an elaboration on Yang Zhu's thought.

Currently, several discussions in academia engage the question whether or not Yang Zhu should be considered a Wei-Jin period scholar. Some argue that the tendency toward indulgence in Yang Zhu was a post-Han phenomenon, but this is clearly not the case. Already Xunzi, in a chapter where he argues explicitly against other thinkers, says, "indulging in sexual desires and resting in recklessness—this is how animals act" (6.2). This shows that such ideas were already in circulation before the Han. Even more importantly, assuming that Yang promoted selfish desires is a superficial reading of his ideas. Like Zhuangzi, Yang Zhu wanted people to be settled in their own individual natures, guided by their own heart-and-minds, and satisfied in their lives.

Liezi

Liezi's original name was Lie Yukou 列御寇. He came from the state of Zheng 郑 (modern Henan). The *Hanshu* records the *Liezi* as having eight chapters, the same as today's version. According to Yan Lingfeng, Liezi was born before 339 BCE (1994); however, much of his work was complied and edited long after his death, and the text bearing his name appears to have been formed much later. Today, there is already a fifty-year-long tradition, started by Liang Qichao, of positing the Liezi as a Wei-Jin period work. Liang gives two major reasons in support of this. First, he argues that there are Buddhist ideas in the text, which were not introduced into China until the Wei-Jin period, including records of "Western sages" that are also supposedly Buddhist. Second, he believes that certain terms, such as *taiyi* 太易 (grand transformation), *taichu* 太初 (grand initiation), *taishi* 太始 (grand beginning), and *taisu* 太素 (grand simplicity) came from another Wei-Jin text, the *Yiwei* 易纬 (Weft of the Changes). These arguments are not entirely reliable.

There is really nothing Buddhist in the *Liezi*. Similar mentions of "Western sages" appear in many pre-Qin texts. The *Shijing* records, "Those beautiful people, the Western people" (1.3.4), and Mozi writes, "King Wen ruled the West" (4.7). These references have nothing to do with Buddhism (see Yan 1969). In additional, the terms Liang thinks came from later Wei-Jin texts are related to concepts already evident in the *Laozi* and *Zhuangzi*. Looking at the *Liezi* and the *Yiwei*, it is clear that the latter copied from the former, and not visa-versa. We can thereby stick to dating the *Liezi* as a pre-Qin text.

Liezi, Laozi, and Zhuangzi are the three major figures of mainstream Daoism. Their ideas about the heavens, Dao, and the organization of the world largely go back to the *Laozi*. Liezi differs from the other two principally in his views on Dao and the concept of self-so. In the "Tianrui" 天瑞 chapter of the *Liezi* (ch. 1), the author discusses the cosmos, arguing that things are constantly transforming and giving birth to one another, which is similar to Laozi and Zhuangzi's thought. All three thinkers emphasize that things change of themselves, and have their own unique characteristics and abilities.

Liezi also talks about the origin of the cosmos, delineating four stages that develop from "without form" to "having form," passing through grand transformation, grand initiation, grand beginning, and grand simplicity. During grand transformation, form (*xing* 形), vital energy (*qi*), and qualities (*zhi* 质) mix together, corresponding to Laozi's declaration that Dao has three aspects that cannot be examined and thereby mix together to form a single undifferentiated entity (ch. 14).

During grand initiation, vital energy emerges fully, while in the course of grand beginning forms take shape. Qualities finally appear in the stage of grand simplicity. This also fits Zhuangzi's account that "during the mixing of various things, there was transformation, which gave rise to vital energy (*qi*); this changed, and there was form; then form changed, and there was life" (11.2). Liezi also maintains that the heavens, the earth, and humanity were formed through the assemblance of vital energy: "The clear and light ascend to the heavens; the dark and heavy descend to the earth" (1.2). This is already a much more specific image of the formation of the world than we have in either the *Laozi* or the *Zhuangzi*. Liezi also supports the idea that humans have a privileged place in the world, which is a major element of his very positive embrace of life—a much more positive perspective on humanity than those of either Laozi or Zhuangzi.

The most exceptional part of Liezi's thinking is his discussion of emptiness. The text describes how he responded to the question of what is valuable about emptiness. He replies that emptiness values nothing and is therefore praiseworthy, then goes on to say, "Without a name, nothing is like stillness, nothing is like emptiness. Stillness and emptiness, that is where it finds residence. Giving and receiving result in loss. When things are broken humanity and duty come into play, and [at that point] things cannot be reversed" (*Liezi* 1.11).

Liezi's "valuing emptiness" is, therefore, a way of maintaining an empty mental state, which allows one to follow along one's own self-so path. This is what Laozi means when he writes, "Emptiness brought to the extreme, stillness carefully guarded. All beings interact in their processes of activity" (ch. 16). Liezi also discusses the limitlessness of the cosmos, writing, "Beyond the limitless is return to the non-limitless; within the endless is return to the non-endless. The limitless returns to the non-limitless; the endless returns to the non-endless" (5.1). The point here is to broaden people's thinking through contemplation of the boundlessness of the cosmos, which is similar in purpose to related concepts in the *Zhuangzi*.

Zhuangzi

Toward the end of the Warring States period there were many Daoist thinkers. The most influential strains, both of their time and historically, were the Zhuangzi, Jixia, and Huang-Lao schools.

The first goes back to Zhuangzi, aka Zhuang Zhou, originally from the city of Meng 蒙 in the state of Song 宋. His text, the *Zhuangzi*, is recorded in the *Hanshu* as having fifty-two chapters. Today only thirty-three chapters remain, divided into Inner, Outer, and Miscellaneous. The first seven form the Inner Chapters, said go back to Zhuang Zhou himself, while students or followers authored the others. The edition we have today, and the classification of the chapters, comes from the Jin dynasty commentator Guo Xiang 郭象 (252-312), who may or may not have significantly altered or edited the text.

After Laozi, Zhuangzi is the most significant pre-Qin Daoist thinker. Sima Qian praises him as having "an understanding that peers into everything, the basis of which recalls Laozi's teachings." From the Inner Chapters it is clear that Zhuangzi inherited Laozi's thought. In the "Dazongshi" chapter (ch. 6), he writes, "Dao has realness and reliability, but no action and no form. It can be conveyed, but it cannot be transmitted. It can be obtained, but not seen. It is its own root, its own foundation. It firmly secured its existence before the heavens and the earth" (6.3). Zhuangzi's Dao, like Laozi's, exists before the heavens and the earth and is beyond the realm of space and time. Zhuangzi, however, further emphasizes Dao's aspects of comprehensive wholeness; he also manages to surpass Laozi in building a complete and unique epistemological system.

Zhuangzi's largest contribution to the development of Laozi's thought is taking the latter's cosmological and ontological Dao and transforming it into a perspective on the heart-and-mind. Zhuangzi's philosophy can accordingly be understood as a philosophy of heart-and-mind horizons. He concentrates on the Dao of humanity, not on Dao as an objective entity. Thus, Zhuangzi completely redevelops some of the characteristics of Dao that Laozi stresses most, such as non-assertive action, reversal, not struggling, softness, weakness, modesty, and downward conduct. Zhuangzi particularly picks up on being self-so, expanding the concept to engage human freedom and new ideas of spontaneity and nonreliance. So, although they are often grouped together, Laozi and Zhuangzi are still significantly different and even opposing in some ways.

The Jixia School and Huang-Lao

During the Warring States period, Huang-Lao thought was popular in the state of Qi, from where it spread to Chu, Qin, and various other states. Its center was the Jixia Academy in Qi, where many scholars authored a number of works (see Hu 1998). Unfortunately, their works have been lost, and all that is left of Jixia Huang-Lao thought is now found in the *Guanzi* (see Chen 2006). Fortunately, Huang-Lao thought as understood in the state of Chu is documented in the *Heguanzi* 鶡冠子

(Pheasant Cap Master); its reading in Qin thought survives in the *Lüshi chunqiu*.

By the latter half of the Warring States, followers of the Spring and Autumn masters were exchanging ideas and fusing various schools of thought. Most traditions other than Zhuangzi's, such as those of the Jixia Academy, Guanzi, and the *Yizhuan*, incorporated Confucian, Mohist, Legalist, School of Names, and Yin-Yang theories into their worldview. Following this pattern, the *Lüshi chunqiu* incorporates an even broader conglomeration of ideas.

In the early 4th century BCE, King Xuan of Qi 齐宣王 gathered scholars from all over the country to discuss academic issues and author scholarly works, covering a broad range of thought. He was hoping to build Qi into a major cultural center and thus founded the Jixia Academy. Bringing together many different thinkers, thought at the Academy incorporated concepts from every school, al though its focus remained on Daoism.

The school's academic endeavors can further be broken down into three branches, each represented by two thinkers: Song Xing 宋钘 and Yin Wen 尹文, Tian Pian 田骈 and Shen Dao 慎到, as well as Huan Yuan 环渊 and Jiezi 接子. According to historical records, Song Xing's thought combines Daoism and Mohism, while Yin Wen's was more like the Huang-Lao school (Hu 1998). The others remained closer to the mainstream Daoism of Laozi and Zhuangzi.

An important document of Jixia ideas, moreover, is the *Guanzi*, and especially its philosophical chapters, "Baixin" 白心, "Neiye" 内业, and "Xinshu" 心术. While the authorship of these chapters is a topic of academic controversy,[2] they are without a doubt products of the Jixia Academy. The *Guanzi* carries forth Laozi's concept of Dao, speaking of emptiness, formlessness, and non-assertive action. It also pioneers major developments of the *Laozi*, however, including in its descriptions of essential energy and the stillness of Dao, which heavily influenced Xunzi (see Wang and Zhou 1983).

As for historical information on major Jixia school representatives, the primary source is the *Shiji*. Huan Yuan, it says, came from the state of Chu, studied Huang-Lao Daoism, and wrote his own two-part text. The *Hanshu* includes a similar record. Unfortunately, Huan's work has been

---

[2] For example, Guo Moruo (1945) thinks that the *Guanzi* was written by Song Xing and Yin Wen, but recently others, such as Zhu Bokun (1989), have argued that it was written by Shen Dao.

lost; however, the *Shiji* notes that he endeavored to order the world and was upset by the chaotic state of China. This type of concern for and desire to influence the world places his thinking close to that of Laozi himself.

Jiezi and Ji Zhen 季真 were, according to Cheng Xuanying, sages from the state of Qi who were part of the Jixia school. The *Hanshu* records the existence of a two-part work called the *Jiezi* 接子 (Book of Master Jie), but mentions no work by Ji Zhen. Very few records of their thought survive. In the *Zhuangzi* and Guo Xiang's commentary no more than a couple of brief sentences mention them, noting only that the two held opposite understandings of the efficacy of Dao's non-assertive action as arising through being or nonbeing.

Peng Meng and Tian Pian, as described in the *Zhuangzi* (ch. 33), were from the state of Qi and participated in the Jixia Academy. Peng Meng supposedly was Tian Pian's teacher. The *Hanshu* says that the *Tianzi* 田子 (Book of Master Tian) consisted of twenty-five chapters; however, these do not survive.

The *Zhuangzi* also says that Peng Meng, Tian Pian, and Shen Dao formed a school of thought within Jixia that principally advocated promoting justice while condemning selfishness and prejudice; maintaining a humane attitude toward all beings; and being self-so and not overthinking or scheming (ch. 33).

Historical records of Peng Meng are very limited. In addition to the *Zhuangzi*, he is mentioned in a dialogue between Tian Pian and Song Xing in the "Tiandao" chapter of the *Yinwenzi*. They discuss China's peaceful state under the rule of the ancient sage-emperor Yao, and describe what Peng Meng thought about the sages: that they should allow things to follow their own self-so paths and that human interference could be disastrous.

Records of Tian Pian are equally scarce. The *Lüshi chunqiu* notes that he valued fairness and saw great equality among the things of the world, that he believed that beings following their own natural tendencies would make everything "appropriate." The commentator Gao You 高诱 further adds that he wrote a work in twenty-five chapters; the *Huainanzi* confirms that he was a close follower of Laozi and a talented scholar.

The *Zhuangzi* also comments on Shen Dao, saying that he also followed Laozi's theory of self-so (ch. 33). The *Shiji* mentions that he authored twelve articles, the *Hanshu* says that he wrote a book of forty-two chapters. Only seven chapters of the *Shenzi* are extant today, and from them we see clearly that he is Daoist (Zhang 1971, 314). Wu Guang argues that "Shen Dao and Tian Pian were similar in that they both were early Daoist thinkers who merged Daoism with Legalist ideas. They differed from Laozi and Zhuangzi in their absorption of Legalist theories of governance. They differed greatly from Legalists like Shang Yang and Han Fei, as well, and therefore cannot be considered Legalists, either. The thrust of their fundamental thinking can best be classified as Daoist" (1985, 85).

The overall thought of Peng Meng, Tian Pian, and Shen Dao is best represented in the concept of "equalizing things"—matching the title of *Zhuangzi*, chapter 2. Shen Dao's theory, however, is not quite the same as Zhuangzi's. Zhuangzi believes in the equality of the voices of every person, every being, and every school, although not in the equal value of their content. Shen's and Tian's understanding of equality establishes an objective standard, which goes on to blur the line between Dao and law. Despite their divergence from it, Shen and Tian's interpretation has had a lasting impact on how Zhuangzi's theory of "equalizing things" is read.

Huangdi sijing and *Heguanzi*

According to the *Shiji*, the philosophies of Shen Dao, Tian Pian, and Huan Yuan include certain elements of Huang-Lao thought. This is also supported by the *Guanzi*. The major characteristics of Huang-Lao involve reworking the understanding of Dao as developed in the *Laozi* by adding elements of Legalism and deriving theories of law arising from Dao. Some scholars have argued that Huang-Lao represents a marriage of Daoist and Legalist thought, which is not accurate. The Huang-Lao school remained rooted in Daoism while absorbing Legalist ideas. Legalism was integrated into the Daoist system, serving as a development of Daoist thought rather than a combination of the two schools.

In the mid-to-late Warring States period, Qi and Chu became meccas for Daoist thinkers. The importance of Daoist theories of politics becomes clear from the works excavated at Mawangdui, a place near modern Changsha in the ancient state of Chu. They include versions of the *Laozi* along with four other texts, the *Jingfa* 经法 (Classic on Method), *Shiliu jing* 十六经 (Sixteen Classics), *Cheng* 称 (Fitting), and *Daoyuan* 道原 (Dao the Fundamental). Tang Lan has shown that these are the four texts referred to as the *Huangdi sijing* in the *Hanshu* (Tang 1975). Their discovery provides great insight into early Huang-Lao thought and its relationship to the Jixia Academy. Therefore, I maintain that the discovery of these four texts is even more important than the versions of the *Laozi* found at Mawangdui.

The *Huangdi sijing* was composed around the time of Mengzi and Zhuangzi. Some have argued, based on the phraseology used, that these four texts were authored between the Qin and Han dynasties. In reality, however, there is nothing about the language in the *Huangdi sijing* that cannot be found in earlier or contemporary texts such as the *Mengzi* or *Zhanguoce*. There is, moreover, no evidence that the *Mengzi* or *Zhuangzi* influenced any of its four books. Indeed, their language seems if anything earlier than that of these texts. Quite significantly, one of the most reliable ways to date a text in Chinese is to look at the number of single character words versus binomials.[3] In the *Huangdi sijing*, the word "Dao" appears eighty-six times and the term "virtuosity" forty-two times, but the compound Dao-virtuosity is never used. Similarly, *jing* 精 appears nine times, and *shen* 神 fourteen, but the word *jingshen* 精神 does not.

The four books of the *Huangdi sijing* contain more than 11,000 characters. Surprisingly, the writing style and content remain consistent throughout, suggesting that they are the work of a single author. Their central discussion of Dao is based on the *Laozi* and describes Dao as a metaphysical entity responsible for constructing the world. Also like the *Laozi*, they tell us that Dao maintains a basic pattern of motion that moves toward extremes and then returns.

In terms of cosmology, the *Huangdi sijing* adopts the position of the *Laozi*. However, when it comes to more practical matters, its texts represent a major development on earlier ideas. Absorbing certain Legalist notions, they argue that law is born from Dao, and like the Mohist tradition, rally against human selfishness. The *Huangdi sijing* thus represents an inclusive school of thought that adopts an even more proactive approach toward society than the *Laozi*. This is shown in four major aspects:

1. Laozi argues that actions should accord with favorable timing. The *Huangdi sijing* presents a more elaborate discussion of mastering expedient conditions, telling us to seize opportunities quickly and that "when the time is right, act, do not speak" (2.2). The text further says, "Sages are not lucky, they know how to follow [the patterns of] time," (2.2). Sima Qian cites this as part of his summary of the Daoist spirit.

2. Laozi is concerned with how to allow the people to prosper of themselves. The *Huangdi sijing* discusses the issue in greater detail.

---

[3] This is the method Liu Xiaogan uses to classify and date the *Zhuangzi* chapters (2010).

3. Laozi warns rulers that being too selfish and attempting to steal from the people puts the state in peril, which leads him to advocate not struggling. This idea, however, remains broad and somewhat vague in the *Laozi*. The *Huangdi sijing* looks closely at struggling and not struggling in a situational context, recognizing the use or necessity of struggling or striving in certain circumstances.

4. Laozi worries that rulers and officials were impatient and cruel, so advocates stillness and softness. However, his perspective is quite extreme, whereas the *Huangdi sijing* gives a much more practical and balanced view of these concepts.

Although the *Huangdi sijing* lacks originality, it develops Daoist theory in a way that makes it compatible with a Confucian society while integrating ideas from a variety of schools of thought, which has had a lasting influence on Daoism's legacy throughout the ages.

Heguanzi was a hermit from the state of Chu. The *Hanshu* records that the *Heguanzi* contained only one chapter, which suggests that most of the transmitted text's nineteen chapters are the work of later writers.

Like the *Huangdi sijing*, the *Heguanzi* both inherits and develops Laozi's discussion of cosmology based on Dao. It discusses the creation of the ten thousand things (i.e. all beings) along the same lines the *Laozi* does, and then introduces the additional concept of "primordial energy," part of Dao from which the world is created.

In terms of social and political philosophy, the *Heguanzi* advocates non-assertive action, but it differs from the *Laozi* by adding Legalist, Mohist, and Confucian ideas. Advocating theories such as "utilizing both virtuosity and virtuosity" and "combining punishment with moral education" colors it strongly with characteristics of Huang-Lao thought.

Laozi's Impact

The close relation between the various schools of pre-Qin thought and Laozi cannot be doubted. He clearly shaped the course of Daoist thought, and also influenced the development of the military, Confucian,[4] and Legal schools. Let us now look at his impact in these traditions.

---

[4] Translator's note: Chen Guying's original Chinese text includes a section, entitled "Laozi's Influence on Pre-Qin Thought." However, this is not included in this translation. The fact that Kongzi, the father of Confucianism, asked Laozi about the rites, has already been thoroughly explained in chapter 1 above. There Chen also shows that Laozi's influence extended other various aspects of

The Military

Many scholars have pointed out the close relationship between the *Laozi* and military thought. During the Tang dynasty, Wang Zhen 王真 said that there is not one sentence in the *Laozi* that does not inform military theory. Later, Wang Fuzhi 王夫之 extolled Laozi's role as teacher of military strategy. In fact, there is quite a lot in the *Laozi* that is explicitly military oriented.

Laozi presents very fundamental views on the military. He writes, "Even the best weapons are inauspicious things, abhorrent to all. Those who know Dao do not use them" (ch. 31). He also says, "An official who is in accord with Dao does not use military means to force the things of the world" (ch. 30). War, however, cannot always be avoided, and so at times there is no alternative but to engage one's enemy, and therefore Laozi also advises on how to do so effectively. He advocates "remaining calm and composed" (ch. 31). Sunzi agrees with this, saying, "Those skilled in using the military can take the enemy's troops without a fight. They can capture other's cities without attacking them. They can ruin a country in a short time" (*Sunzi bingfa* 3.3). Even though Sunzi is a great military strategist, he still thinks that one should only attack when there is no other choice.

Laozi's guiding principle for war is to "use soldiers in an unpredictable manner" (ch. 57) He describes this more specifically:

> I dare not host the battle—I am merely its guest [on the defensive].
> I dare not advance an inch—I retreat a foot.
> This is called preparing the ranks when there are none:
> Baring no arms, holding no weapons, and advancing on no enemy.
> The worst calamity is taking war too lightly;
> Taking war too lightly means almost losing that which is precious to me.
> Thus, when crossing weapons, those loath to do so shall triumph. (ch. 69)

This approach further includes his theory that "the soft and weak overcome the hard and strong" (ch. 36). When Laozi speaks of "using soldiers in an unpredictable manner," this involves residing in the weak and staying on the defensive. Sunzi similarly states:

Kongzi's thought, as well as to latter Confucian texts, especially the *Daxue* and *Zhongyong*.

> For war, direct [methods] are used for joining [the battle], unpredictable [methods] are used for winning. Therefore, those who are good at unpredictable methods are endless [in power], like the heavens and earth, and are inexhaustible [in fighting] like the flowing rivers and streams. (5.2)

> The way to conduct war is to be deceptive. Therefore, when able [to attack] show that you are unable. Use [forces] but show that you are not using [forces]. Close in, but appear to be far, when far appear to be close. Display a beneficial situation to lure the enemy, feign disorder, and take the enemy.
>
> If the enemy is secure, buckle down, if the enemy is strong, avoid them. When the enemy is irritated, annoy them. Feign weakness to make them arrogant. When they rest, do work [against them]. If they are close to one another, break them up.
>
> Attack when they are not prepared, come from where you are least expected, this is [the way of the] winners, and [these tactics] cannot be told first [one must experience them, as well]. (*Sunzi bingfa* 1.6)

These two passages clearly show that Sunzi agreed with Laozi's advice to "use soldiers in an unpredictable manner" (ch. 57) and even expanded on this theory to develop a strategy based largely on trickery and deception.

Legalism

Although Laozi was opposed to ordering the state through strict laws, many of his other theories were picked up by Legalist thinkers. The *Shiji* contains a chapter that records the life of Laozi alongside those of Han Feizi and Shen Buhai 申不害, two of the most prominent pre-Qin Legalist thinkers, presumably because of the close relationship between the two schools.

As a school of thought, Legalism was a late bloomer, and thereby took on theories from a diversity of other schools, but none more so than from the Daoists. Shen Dao blurred the line between the Legalism and Daoism, while the Shen Buhai and Han Feizi based themselves strongly in Huang-Lao. The *Hanfeizi* in fact includes two chapters expounding on the *Laozi*, highlighting the intimate connection between the two schools. Legalism furthermore inherited the concept of non-assertive action. Han writes:

> The ruler should maintain an empty and still mentality, which makes people naturally do [what they are supposed to]. . . . Everything has its proper use, and when things take their appropriate positions, successful govern-

> ance arises through non-assertive action. Like roosters heralding daybreak and cats chasing mice, with everything following its own capacity, rulers create effective order through non-assertive action. (8.1-2)

Here Legalism accords with the *Laozi* in being subjective, advocating equality, and adapting laws to the times and circumstances. There exist many other points of similarity as well. Both philosophize about politics from the perspective of the ruler, focus on grasping foundational issues, and believe in people sticking to their own paths. Other ideas from Laozi seem to find related though not analogous concepts in Legalism, such as hiding the state's most powerful "weapons" and advocating the selflessness of rulers.

The *Lüshi chunqiu*

The *Hanshu* classifies the *Lüshi chunqiu* and the *Huainanzi*—two great comprehensive overviews of early Chinese thought—as mixed compilations of miscellaneous schools. This is not accurate because these texts do not merely throw together elements of various schools of thought; they have dominant frameworks that direct their selection.

Already in the Han dynasty, Gao You asserted that the *Lüshi chunqiu* aims to explain Dao and virtuosity, and focuses on advocating non-assertive action. He further insists that the *Huainanzi* is close to Laozi's thought in its attention to non-assertive action, emptiness, stillness, and Dao. In other words, Gao You explicitly points out that these texts are largely Daoist.

Recently, many academics have also argued against classifying these texts as mixed compilations of works from miscellaneous schools. Mou Zhongjian asserts that these "two books are Daoist works from the transition between the Qin and Han dynasties"(1996); Xiong Tieji believes that they are "representative of 'Neo-Daoism.'" (1984). He further argues that they embrace Laozi and Zhuangzi's philosophies, using them as the basis for synthesizing other schools of thought. Claiming they are representative of the trends of Daoist thought in Qin and Han times, Xiong points out that while they adopt elements of Confucianism, Legalism, and Mohism when focusing on political, economical and cultural issues, they stick to the cosmology and epistemology of the *Laozi* and *Zhuangzi*. On this basis, let us examine the relationship between those two preeminent Daoist works and the *Lüshi chunqiu* more closely.

According to the *Lüshi chunqiu*, the world was formed by a collection of materials, the lighter ones becoming the sky and heavier ones descending and creating the earth:

> The beginning of the heavens and the earth happened thus: subtle things formed the heavens and turbid things formed the earth. The heavens and the earth came together harmoniously, and produced [all] things. This is known by the alternation of seasons, the sun, the moon, as well as night and day. It can be explained by the specific shapes and capabilities of each thing (13.1)

The description here is basically the same as that in the *Liezi* (and also the *Huainanzi*). The detailed images are based on a foundational understanding of the heavens, the patterns of the seasons, the transformation of things, and the formation of the cosmos as derived from the philosophies of Laozi and Zhuangzi. Remarking directly on the constant pattern of renewal, the *Lüshi chunqiu* states, "The heavens and the earth are like a cart wheel, at the end [of a rotation] beginning again, at the apex starting the return" (5.2). This cyclical pattern is based on the *Laozi*'s teaching that "all beings interact in their processes of activity, then I see them return. Things that flourish all return to their roots" (ch. 16).

The *Lüshi chunqiu* also rejects the idea of a "creator." It states, "All beings appear, made from Great Unity [*taiyi* 太一] and changing according to yin and yang" (5.2). "Great Unity," responsible for creating all beings, is a reference to Laozi's Dao. The term first appeared in the *Zhuangzi* and refers to the source of all beings.

In terms of human relationships, the *Lüshi chunqiu* looks to the *Laozi*'s idea of "following the heavens and the earth" as a model (2.3). However, it also explicitly says that people should act in line with the development of things and situations. They should change according to the same patterns as their surroundings and reject selfish desires or notions. When people act in such a way, they can be successful.

In terms of natural philosophy, the *Lüshi chunqiu* was heavily influenced by the Jixia Academy. The text borrows its concept of "essential *qi*" from the *Guanzi*, and its epistemology shows clear marks of Jixia thinkers Song Xing and Yin Wen in its calls for the removal of subjective bias and preconceptions.

The *Lüshi chunqiu*'s life philosophy goes back to Yang Zhu, Laozi, and Zhuangzi. In the "Bensheng" 本生 (1.2), "Zhongji" 重己 (1.3), and "Guisheng" 贵生 (2.2) chapters, Yang Zhu's attitude of "valuing life over things" plays a major role. Many Zhuangzi ideas appear, as well, especially regarding connectedness to the heavens and inherent individual stendencies, as does Laozi's advice regarding long life, correcting one's self before ordering the world, and following natural patterns.

The "Guigong" 贵公 chapter outlines the text's political philosophy. It tells us, "The world is not the world of a single person; it is the world of the world" (1.4.2). This is reminiscent of the *Laozi* and *Zhuangzi*'s quasi-democratic thinking. Just after this cite, a story is told that demonstrates the *Lüshi chunqiu*'s preference for Daoism:

> It has been said, "A person from the state of Chu lost a bow, so someone is the state of Chu got a bow. Why should the one who lost it look for it?" When Kongzi heard this he said "Get rid of the word 'Chu' and this is correct."
>
> When Lao Dan heard the story he said "Get rid of the word 'person' and it is correct." Therefore, Lao Dan reaches the utmost of fairness. The heavens and earth are vast. They give birth to life without regarding anything as a child; the make things without regarding them as possessions. Everything...benefits from the world, even if they do not know it. (1.4)

Despite the frequency with which Kongzi's name appears, it is clear that the *Lüshi chunqiu* favors Laozi's thinking, at one point even explicitly elevating Laozi over Kongzi as his teacher.

Conclusion

Overall, Laozi and his text had a significant impact on the development of all major schools of thought during the Warring States period. His impact on Kongzi can be seen clearly in the *Lunyu*; his role in Sunzi's military thought is evident from the large part he takes from Laozi's ideas.

In the later Warring States period, Laozi's Daoism broke into two schools, the Zhuangzi school and the Jixia school. Though separate, they developed together through healthy communication. Philosophically, the Zhuangzi school became exceptional in essentially all aspects, while the Jixia school proved very influential politically. Together with the Huang-Lao tradition, these strands of Daoism formed the peak of intellectual thought and continued to develop until the end of the Warring States period, when they were fused together in the *Lüshi chunqiu*. This text primarily took from the thought of Laozi, Zhuangzi, and the Huang-

Lao tradition, but absorbed Yin-Yang, Confucian, Mohist, School of Names, and Legalist ideas, as well.

Xu Fuguan (1963) argues that Daoism lasted as a major current of thought for over four hundred years, and that the flourishing of Huang-Lao thought at the beginning of the Han inherited that tradition. From the above, it is clear that the many schools of Daoism had a broad impact on early Chinese thought. Most contemporary scholars understand Confucianism as the surface of traditional Chinese culture, with Daoism forming its core. The paramount role of Daoism in early Chinese philosophy is verified in ancient texts.

Xiao Shafu (1998) explains that the "Tianxia" chapter of the *Zhuangzi* mentions eight major schools of thought, four of which are Daoist. In other words, half of the leading academic schools were Daoist. The *Xunzi* and *Shizi* 尸子 (Book of Shi Jiao) each list six major schools, and both include three Daoist ones. The *Lüshi chunqiu* discusses ten schools, five of which are considered Daoist. Daoism's dominance of pre-Qin thought is incontestable. Whether we look at the number of schools or the quality of their thought, Daoism conclusively forms the backbone of pre-Qin philosophy.

Bibliography

Cai Yuanpei 蔡元培. 1970. *Zhongguo lunli xueshi* 中国伦理学史 (A History of Chinese Ethics). Guilin: Guangxi Normal University Publishing.

Chen Guying 陈鼓应. 1988. "Laoxue xianyu kongxue" 老学先于孔学 (Laozi Precedes Kongzi). *Zhexue yanjiu* 哲学研究: 180-201.

_____. 2002. "Laozi yu Kongzi sixiang bijiao yanjiu" 老子与孔子思想比较研究 (A Comparison of Laozi and Kongzi's Thought).

_____. 2006. *Guanzi sipian quanshi* 管子四篇诠释 (An Explanation of the *Guanzi*). Shanghai: Shangwu.

_____ 2007. *Huangdi sijing jinzhu jinshi: Mawangdui Hanmu boshu* 黄帝四经今 注今译：马王堆汉墓帛书. Beijing: Shangwu.

_____. 2011. *Daojia wenhua yanjiu* 道家文化研究 (Studies on Daoist Culture). Beijing: Sanlian.

Chen Jinsheng 陈金生. 1982. "Zhouyi yu Zhongguo zhexue" 周易与中国哲学 (The *Zhouyi* and Chinese Philosophy). *Wenshi* 文史 14.

Copleston, Frederick Charles. 1993. *A History of Philosophy*. New York: Doubleday.

Cui Shu 崔述. 1983. "*Cui Dongbi yishu* 崔东壁遗书 (The Lost Works of Cui Dongbi). Shanghai: Guji.

Ding Yuanzhi 丁原植. 1999. *Wenzi xinlun* 文子新论 (New Discussions on the *Wenzi*). Taipei: EBSCO.

Fan Wenlan 范文澜. 1954. *Zhongguo tongshi jianbian* 中国通史简编 (A Concise History of China). Beijing: Renmin.

Feng Youlan 冯友兰. 1986. *Zhongguo zhexue shi xinbian* 中国哲学史新编 (A New History of Chinese Philosophy). Beijing: Renmin.

_____. 1997. *A Short History of Chinese Philosophy*. Translated by Derk Bodde. Detroit: Free Press.

_____. 2007. *Xin yuanren* 新原人 (New Discussions on the Original State of Humans). Beijing: Sanlian.

Gao Heng 高亨.1963. "Kongzi sixiang sanlun" 孔子思想三论 (Three Theories on Kongzi's Thought). *Zhexue yanjiu* 哲学研究 1.

_____.1979. "Guanyu Laozi de jige wenti" 关于老子的几个问题 (On a Few Issues in the *Laozi*). In *Shehui kexue zhanqian* 社会科学战线, 1-27.

_____.2011. *Laozi: zhenggu* 老子正诂 (The Proper Commentaries to the *Laozi*). Beijing: Qinghua daxue.

Gao Ming 高明. 1996. *Boshu Laozi jiaozhu* 帛书老子校注 (Commentary on the Guodian *Laozi*). Beijing: Zhonghua.

Gu Xiegang 顾颉刚, ed. 1941. *Gushi bian* 古史辨 (Clarifying Ancient Texts). Shanghai: Guji.

Guo Moruo 郭沫若. 1945. *Qingtong shidai* 青铜时代 (The Bronze Age). Chongqing: Wenzhi.

Hegel, Georg Wilhelm Friedrich. 1995 [1987]. *Lectures on the Philosophy of Religion. Volume II: Determinate Religion*. Edited by Peter C. Hodgson; translated by R. F. Brown, et al.. Berkeley: University of California Press.

Hou Wailu 侯外庐. 1998. *Zhongguo gudai sixiang xueshuo shi* 中国古代思想学说史. Liaoning: Liaoning jiaoyu.

_____, and Huang Xuanmin 黄宣民. 1981. *Zhongguo sixiang shigang* 中国思想史纲 (An Outline of the History of Chinese Thought). Beijing: Zhongguo qingnian.

_____, Zhao Jibin 赵纪彬, and Du Guoxiang 杜国庠. 1957. *Zhongguo sixiang tongshi* 中国思想通史 (A History of Chinese Thought). Beijing: Renmin.

Hu Jiacong 胡家聪. 1998. *Jixia zhengming yu Huang-Lao xinxue* 稷下争鸣与黄老新学 (The Jixia Academy Debates and the Huang-Lao School). Beijing: Zhongguo shehui kexue.

Hu Shi 胡适. 1989. *Zhongguo gudai zhexue shi* 中国古代哲学史 (History of Ancient Chinese Philosophy. Hefei: Anhui jiaoyu.

Hu Zhikui 胡志奎. 1983. *Lunyu bianzheng* 论语辩证 (Dialectics in the *Analects*). Taipei: Liangjing.

Huang Fanggang 黄方刚. 1941. "Laozi niandai zhi kaozheng" 老子年代之考证 (Textual Research on [Texts Written During] Laozi's Time). In *Gushi bian* 古史辨 (Clarifying Ancient Texts), edited by Gu Xiegang 顾颉刚. Shanghai: Guji.

Huang Yongnian 黄永年, ed. 2011. *Han Yu shiwen xuan*responsibility 韩愈诗文选译 (Selections and Intepreations of Han Yu's Poems). Nanjing: Fenghuang.

Jiang Guobao 蒋国保. 2009. *Fang Yizhi yu Ming-Qing zhexue* 方以智与明清哲学 (The Philosophy of Fang Yizhi and the Ming and Qing Dynasties). Anhui: Huangshan.

Li Du 李杜. 1980. *Zhongxi zhexue sixiang zhong de tiandao yu shangdi* 中西哲学思想中的天道与上帝 (The Way of Heaven and the Absolute in Chinese and Western Philosophical Thought). Taipei: Liangjing.

Li Jingde 黎靖德, ed. 1986. *Zhuzi yulei* 朱子语类 (Zhu Xi's Sayings). Beijing: Zhonghua.

Li Taicai 李泰菜. 1958. *Lao-Zhuang yanjiu* 老庄研究 (Studies on the *Laozi* and *Zhuangzi*). Beijing: Renmin.

Li Xueqin 李学勤. 1981. *Chu wenhua xintan* 楚文化新探 (New Investigations on the Culture of Chu). Wuhan: Hubei renmin.

Li Zehou 李泽厚. 1986. *Zhongguo gudai sixiang shilun* 中国古代思想史论 (Historical Discussions of Ancient Chinese Thought). Beijing: Renmin.

Liang Qichao 梁启超. 1941. "Lun Laozi shu zuoyu Zhanguo zhimo" 论老子书作于战国之末" (On the *Laozi* Being Composed in the Late Warring States). In *Gush bian* 古史辨 (Clarifying Ancient Texts), edited by Gu Xiegang 顾颉刚. Shanghai: Guji.

_____梁启超. 2009. *Zhongguo lishi yanjiu fa* (Methods of Researching Chinese History). Beijing: Zhonghua.

Liu Xianmei 刘先枚. 1986. "Lun nanfang zhi xue yu beifang zhi xue de bianzheng fazhang"论南方之学与北方之学的辩证发展 (Textual Analysis of the Development of the Northern and Southern Schools of Thought). In *Zhouyi zongheng lu* 周易纵横录 (Various Records Concerning the Book of Changes), edited by Tang Mingbang 唐明邦 and Luo Chi 罗炽. Wuhan: Hubei renmin.

Liu Xiaogan 刘笑敢. 2010. *Zhuangzi zhexue jiqi yanbian* 庄子哲学及其演变 (The Philosophy of the *Zhuangzi* and its Evolution). Beijing: Renmin daxue.

Lu Yusan 卢育三. 1987. *Laozi shiyi* 老子释义 (Discussing the *Laozi*). Tianjin: Tianjin guji.

Luo Genze 罗根泽. "Zhanguo qian wusi jia zhuzuo shuo" 战国前无私家著作说 (A Theory of No Individual Authors in Pre-Warring States Times). In *Gushi bian* 古史辨 (Clarifying Ancient Texts), edited by Gu Xiegang 顾颉刚. Shanghai: Guji.

Ma Xulun 马叙伦. 1974. *Laozi jiaogu* 老子校诂 (The *Laozi* and Selected Commentaries). Beijing: Zhonghua.

Mawangdui 马王堆汉墓帛书整理小组编. 1974. *Mawangdui Hanmu boshu, yi* 马王堆汉墓帛书(壹). Taipei: Wenwu.

Mou Zhongjian 牟钟鉴. 1996. *Zhongguo daojiao* 中国道教 (Chinese Daoism). Guangzhou: Guangdong renmin.

Nietzsche, Friedrich. 2001. *The Gay Science: With a Prelude in German and an Appendix of Songs*. Edited by Bernard Williams; translated by Josefine Nauckhoff and Adrian Del Caro. Cambridge: Cambridge University Press.

Pang Pu 庞朴. 1984. *Rujia bianzheng fa yanjiu* 儒家辩证法研究 (Studies in Confucian Dialectics). Beijing: Zhonghua.

Qian Mu 钱穆. 2005. *Laozhuang tongbian* 老庄通辨 (An Explanation of Laozi and Zhuangzi's Thought). Beijing: Sanlian.

Ren Jiyu 任继愈, ed. 1979a. *Zhongguo zhexue shi lunwen ji* 中国哲学史论文集 (A Collection of Essays on the History of Chinese Philosophy). Jinan: Shandong renmin.

_____.1979b."Zhongguo gudai zhexue fazhan de diqu xing" 中国古代哲学发展的地区性 (The Regional Nature of the Development of Ancient Chinese Philosophy. In *Zhongguo zhexue shi lunwen ji* 中国哲学史论文集 (A Collection of Essays on the History of Chinese Philosophy), edited by Ren Jiyu 任继愈. Jinan: Shandong renmin.

Tang Junyi 唐君毅. 1986. *Zhongguo zhexue yuanlun* 中国哲学原论 (A Theory of Chinese Philosophy). Taipei: Xuesheng.

Tang Mingbang 唐明邦, and Luo Chi 罗炽, eds. 1986. *Zhouyi zongheng lu* 周易纵横录 (Various Records Concerning the Book of Changes). Wuhan: Hubei renmin.

Tong Shuye 童书业. 1982. *Xianqin qizi sixiang yanjiu* 先秦七子思想研究 (A Study of Seven Masters During Pre-Qin Times). Jinan: Jilu.

Tu Youguang 涂又光. 1995. *Chuguo zhexue shi* 楚国哲学史 (The History of Philosophy in the State of Chu). Wuhan: Hubei jiaoyu.

Wang Bo 王博. 1989. "Laozi yu xiazu wenhua" 老子与夏族文化 (Laozi and Xia Dynasty Culture). *Zhexue yanjiu* 1.

Wang Huanbio 王焕镳. 2005. *Mozi jiaoshi* 墨子校释 (The *Mozi* with Commentary and Interpretations). Shanghai: Guji.

Wang Qixing 王启星. 1986. "Jianlun rujia shijiao de yingxiang" 简论儒家诗教的影响 (A Brief Discussion on the Influence of Confucian Poetry). *Guangming ribao* 光明日报 1986.

Wang Xiaobo 王晓波. 1984. *Rufa sixiang lunji* 儒法思想论集 (A Collection of Essays on Confucian and Legalist Thought). Taipei: Taipei shibao wenhua.

Xiao Gongquan 萧公权, and Li Jinquan 李锦全. 2005. *Zhongguo zhengzhi sixiang shi* 中国政治思想史 (A History of Chinese Political Thought). Beijing: Xinxing.

Xiao Shafu 萧萐父. 1998. *Zhongguo zhexue shi shiliao yuanshu juyao* 中国哲学史史料源流举要 (The Historical Origin of Chinese Philosophy). Wuhan: Wuhan daxue.

Xiong Tieji 熊铁基. 1984. *Qin-Han xin daojia luelun gao* 秦汉新道家略论稿 (On Qin and Han Dynasty Daoist Philosophy). Shanghai: Renmin.

Xu Fuguan 徐复观. 1963. *Zhongguo* humaneness*xing lun shi* 中国人性论史 (The History of Discussions on Human Tendencies in Chinese Thought). Taipei: Donghai daxue.

Yan Lingfeng 严灵峰. 1969. *Wuqiu beizhai xueshu lunji* 无求备斋学术论集 (Collected Studies of Wuqiu Beizhai). Taipei: Zhonghua.

______. 1994. *Liezi bianwu jiqi zhongxin sixiang* 列子辩诬及其中心思想 (Central Ideas and Debates on the *Liezi*). Jinan: Wenshizhe.

Ye Liang 叶亮. 1985. *Zhongguo meixue shi dagang* 中国美学史大纲 (An Outline History of Chinese Aesthetics). Shanghai: Shanghai renmin.

Yu Jiaxi 余嘉锡. 1985. *Gushu tonglie* 古书通例 (General Practices of Ancient Texts). Shanghai: Guji.

Zhan Jianfeng 詹剑锋. 1982. *Laozi qiren qishu ji qidao lun* 老子其人其书及其道论 (Discussion of Laozi—Man, Book, and Dao). Wuhan: Hubei renmin.

Zhang Chunyi 张纯一. 1936. *Mozi jijie* 墨子集解(Collected Works of Mozi). Shanghai: Shijie.

Zhang Dainian 张岱年.1958. *Zhongguo zhexue dagang* 中国哲学大纲 (An Outline of Chinese Philosophy). Shanghai: Shangwu.

______. 1979. "*Laozi zhexue bianwei* 老子哲学辨微 (Analysis of Differences in Laozi's Philosophy). In *Zhongguo zhexue shi lunwen ji* 中国哲学史论文集 (A Collection of Essays on the History of Chinese Philosophy), edited by Ren Jiyu. Jinan: Shandong renmin.

_____.1992. "*Sunzi bingfa*" 孙子兵法 (Sunzi's Art of War). *Sunzi xuekan* 孙子学刊 1.

Zhang Guangzhi 张光直. 1983. *Zhongguo qingtong ahidai* 中国青铜时代 (China's Bronze Age). Beijing: Sanlian.

Zhang Xu 张煦. 1941. "Liang rengong tisu Laozi shidai yi an panjue shu" 梁任公提诉《老子》时代一案判决书 (A Judgment on Liang's Case for the *Laozi*'s Time Period). In *Gushi bian* 古史辨 (Clarifying Ancient Texts), edited by Gu Xiegang 顾颉刚. Shanghai: Guji Publishing 古籍出版社.

Zhou Lisheng 周立升, and Wang Demin 王德敏. 1983. "Guanzi zhong de jingqi lun jiqi lizhi gongxian" 管子中德精气及其历久贡献 (The Argument of Vital Essences and the Historical Contribution of the *Guanzi*). *Zhexue yanjiu* 哲学研究 5.

Zhu Bokun 朱伯昆. 1989. *Guanzi de guojia guanli xueshuo* 管子的国家管理学说 (The *Guanzi*'s Theory of National Management). Singapore: Dongya zhexue yanjiu suo.

Index

being, *see* nonbeing
Bian Shao, 6
Bo Qin, 33
Buddhism, 12, 28, 69, 79, 109, 116,
Cai Yuanpei, 32, 55
Chen Jinsheng, 29
Cheng Xuanying, 112, 120
Chuci, 33
Dao: as being, 42-43, 75, 78-80, 89-91, 108, 109-10, 120; concept of, 5, 27, 37-46, 49, 61, 65, 72, 78-80, 81, 83-84, 87-90, 95-96, 105-06, 108, 110, 113, 118, 122-23, 126-27; and *de*, 1, 17, 38, 44-45, 53, 59, 83, 87, 91, 95, 113, 122, 126; emptiness of, 10, 23-24, 89-90, 100-02, 106, 109, 112, 118-19, 126; fullness of, 8, 10, 41, 44; of the heavens, 4-5, 27, 38-43, 46, 49, 61, 69, 120; and Kongzi, 6, 30, 43-45, 61; and law, 78, 121-22; method(s) of, 24-25, 27, 36, 41, 47, 53, 75-76, 92, 98, 103; and "middle", 75-77; as nonbeing, 42, 75, 78-80, 91, 108, 110, 120; as "not-struggling," 36, 103-05, 112, 118; and personal cultivation, 24, 43, 46-47 59, 67, 70, 75-78, 80-84, 87-88, 95-100, 106, 124; and political order, 24, 27, 30, 36-37, 43-45, 47, 53, 70-71, 77-78, 88, 96, 98-99, 105-06, 121-22, 124; and *qi*, 43, 112, 116; as reversal/cyclical, 8, 39-42, 92, 94-96, 108, 122; and self-so/non-assertive action, 25, 37-42, 46-47, 61, 71, 83-4, 95-100, 106, 116, 118-20, 126; stillness of, 47, 59, 75-6, 100-02, 106, 108, 118-19, 126; and yin-yang, 41-43
Daxue, 38, 124
Deng Xi, *see Zhuxing*
Dong Zhongshu, 12
Duke of Zhou, 34, 81
Duty, *see* responsibility
Fan Li, 16-17, 41, 65
Fan Wenlan, 35
Feng Youlan, 1, 13-6, 21, 28, 31, 33, 38, 39, 54, 56, 60-61, 80-81, 83,
Fromm, Erich, 54
Gao Heng, 6, 50
Gongsun Long, 5
Guan Yin, 112
Guanzi, 15-16, 44, 65, 75, 77, 89, 111, 118-19, 121, 127
Guodian, 63-68, 70-71, 74-75, 78-80, 82, 86
Guoyu, 16, 18, 41, 54-55
Hanfeizi, 9, 70, 125
harmony, 31, 37, 41, 45, 46, 70-71, 75-7, 87
Hanshu, 33, 112-15, 117, 119-21, 123, 126
Han Yu, 12
heart-and-mind, 25, 36, 49, 57, 59, 70, 75-77, 83-84, 102, 112-13, 115, 118
Hegel, G.W.F.: on Chinese history, 30; dialectics in, 18, 21-2, 28
Heguanzi, 118, 121, 123
Hu Shi, 2, 11, 13-15, 28, 81, 98
Huainanzi, 10, 23, 26, 92, 114-15, 120, 126-27
Huang Fanggang, 6, 11-12
Huang-Lao, 16, 74-78, 109, 111, 117-19, 121, 123, 125, 128-29

Hui Shi, 5
humaneness, 5, 11, 18, 22, 26-28, 52, 54-58, 60-61, 63, 68-74, 80, 82-87, 98, 106, 113
Jiezi, 119-20
Jixia Academy, 15, 43, 75, 77, 111, 113, 117-21, 127-28
Ji Zhen, 120
Kongzi, 1-2, 4-5, 35, 65, 128
Ku county, 1-2, 7
Lao Dan (Laozi): and *Daode jing*, 2, 4, 9, 13, 29, 37, 65-66, 111-13; and Kongzi, 1-2, 4-5, 35, 65, 128; and the *Zhuangzi*, 71, 112,
Laolaizi, 3, 13, 17, 34
Laozi ming, 6
Legalism, 121, 125-26
Li Daoyuan, 6
Li Er, 2-3, 13
Li Taicai, 11
Liang Qichao, 1, 3-4, 6-7, 11, 57, 65, 116
Lie Yukou, *see* Liezi
Liji, 4-9, 16, 51, 54, 65
Lüshi chunqiu, 4-6, 9, 16, 65, 111, 115, 119-20, 126-29
Lu Yusan, 41
Luo Genze, 1, 17
Ma Xulun, 11, 13
Mawangdui, 14, 63-64, 66-67, 78, 121-22
Mao Zedong, 15
ming, 26, 39, 46
Mozi, 10, 13-15, 19, 22-29, 56, 64-65, 85, 113-14, 116
Mozi jijie, 24
nature, 19-20, 25, 30-31, 32-34, 37-42, 45-49, 52-54, 58-59, 61, 71-72, 76, 83, 87, 91-98, 100-01, 103, 106, 108, 111, 113, 115, 120, 126-28
Nietzsche, Friedrich, 49, 54, 57
nonbeing, 42, 63, 75, 78, 79, 80-81, 90-93, 107-10, 120
non-assertive action, 11, 23, 25, 37, 39, 42, 46-47, 54, 84, 96, 98-100, 102-03, 112, 119-20, 123, 125-26
Pengzu, 10-11
petty people, 36-37, 40, 44-45
qi, 40, 112, 116-17, 127
Qian Mu, 28-29, 63, 65,
responsibility, 4, 18, 22, 28, 52, 63, 68-75, 80, 82-87, 113
reversal, 12-14, 92, 94-95, 99, 103, 117-18
Ren Jiyu, 33
rites, 1, 3-4, 6, 8, 13, 18-20, 26-27, 38, 43-45, 48-52, 54, 57-58, 60, 69-70, 72, 83, 87, 103, 113
self-so, 19, 31, 37-8, 40, 42, 45-46, 61, 83, 96-98, 100, 105-06, 112, 115, 117-18, 120-21
Shangshu, 4, 8, 39, 54
Shen Buhai, 125
Shenzi, 15, 65, 120
Shiji, 1-3, 6-7, 11, 17-18, 24, 37, 56, 130, 136-38, 143
Shijing, 4, 8, 13, 39, 60, 116
Shuoyuan, 9
Sima Qian, 1-4, 17, 23, 66, 118, 122
Suishu, 112
Sunzi bingfa, 9, 13-14, 16-17, 29, 124-25
Taiyi shengshui, 63-64, 80
Taiping yulan, 9-10, 22, 24,
Tianzi, 120
Tong Shuye, 56
Tu Youguang, 38
virtuosity (*de*), see Dao
Wang Bi, 68, 75, 79, 91, 93, 109-10,
Wang Bo, 26, 34, 67
Wang Qixing, 60
Wang Xiaobo, 52
Wang Zhen, 124
Wei-Jin period, 14, 19-21, 75, 79, 81, 115-16
Wei Mou, 5, 20
wisdom, 67-68, 83, 86, 113

Wu Guang, 120
Xiao Gongquan, 51
Xuanxue, 75
Xunzi, 9, 20, 38, 48, 111, 113, 115, 119, 129
Xu Fuguan, 5, 13, 92, 129
Yan Ruoju, 6
Yang Zhu, 19-20, 111, 114-15, 127
Yao Nai, 10
Yijing, 4, 8, 18, 29, 39, 109
Yinwenzi, 15, 120
Yizhuan, 43, 58-59, 119
yin-yang: and Dao, 41-43, 127; ideology/concept of, 41; movement of, 43, 127; and sage, 114; school of, 5, 41, 119
Yu Jiaxi, 20, 66
Zhanguoce, 9-10, 122
Zhongyong, 9-10, 54, 124
Zhuangzi, 4-9, 14, 16, 20-22, 29, 31, 33, 39, 43-44, 46, 49, 59, 65, 68-69, 71-74, 76-77, 83-86, 109, 111-12, 114-122, 126-29
Zhan Jianfeng, 14
Zhang Chunyi, 24-26
Zhang Dainian, 9, 11
Zhang Guangzhi, 32
Zhang Xu, 14, 18
Zhang Zhihan, 15
Zhongxin zhi dao, 80
Zhongguo zhexue xinbian, 81
Zhu Xi, 12, 43, 85
Zhuxing, 13, 17, 50
Zuozhuan, 7, 18, 40-41, 47, 50-51, 53-54